Sunday Morning:
A Time for Worship

SUNDAY MORNING:

A TIME FOR WORSHIP

Edited by

Mark Searle

THE LITURGICAL PRESS—Collegeville, Minnesota

1982

Papers from the Tenth Annual Conference of the Notre Dame Center for Pastoral Liturgy, University of Notre Dame, June 15–18, 1981. The Center for Pastoral Liturgy was established at the University of Notre Dame in 1971 to promote the liturgical life of the Church in North America. Drawing upon the resources of the university, it represents part of the university's effort to serve the wider community through its Center for Pastoral and Social Ministry, of which the Center for Pastoral Liturgy is a component.

Nihil obstat: Robert C. Harren, J.C.L., *Censor deputatus.*
Imprimatur: ✠ George H. Speltz, D.D., Bishop of St. Cloud. March 10, 1982.
Printed in the United States of America.
Cover design by Fred Petters.

Library of Congress Cataloging in Publication Data

Notre Dame Center for Pastoral Liturgy.
   Sunday morning.

   Contents: The origins of Sunday in the New Testament / Eugene LaVerdiere — Sunday Assembly in the tradition / Robert Hovda — Sunday in the Eastern tradition / Robert Taft — [etc.]
   1. Sunday—Congresses. 2. Catholic Church—Liturgy—Congresses. I. Searle, Mark, 1941–
BV111.N67 1982   263'.4   82-15306
ISBN 0-8146-1259-8 (pbk.)   AACR2

Contents

Introduction

MARK SEARLE

The most important thing about Sunday is that, like Christianity itself, it survives as we approach the second millenium. Whether the role of Sunday in the lives of Christians is all that it might be is another question; but it cannot be answered simply by making comparisons with the past, for the circumstances of the age in which we live are vastly different from those that have preceded us. The question of the strength of the Christian Sunday today is significant not in terms of how we measure up to the past, but in terms of the responsibility we have for the future. "We can justly consider," proclaims Vatican II's Constitution on the Church in the Modern World, "that the future of humanity lies in the hands of those who are strong enough to provide coming generations with reasons for living and hoping" (31). The future of the Christian Sunday, it might be argued, lies in its ability to shape Christian life and sustain Christian hope.

Sunday is not merely a day in the week: it is a sacrament of Christian existence. As such, it gathers to itself the central images of Christianity: the encounter with the risen Christ, the experience of God's lordship over time and history, the assembly of the faithful for the celebration of word and sacrament, the fitful yet ultimately assured emergence of a new creation, the relief of human beings liberated from the demonic powers of this world, and the hope (already realized in part) of the blissful communion of a redeemed humanity in the life of God in the age to come. Its very richness defies the narrow compass of our minds and calls into question the often negative stereotypes of so-called Sunday observance. For there is a perversity manifest in the history of the Christian Sunday which has transmuted a sublime gift into a narrow obligation, a day of liberation into a sabbatarian burden, a day for celebrating the words of God into a day off in the round of human toil. But at least it survives, and while it survives it yet holds out the hope that we may still recover the hope it contains.

If Sunday is, indeed, a sacrament of Christian existence, a sacrament of God's transformation of human history, then it both stands in continuity with the rest of time and emerges out of it to point to the ultimate meaning of time itself. Like all the sacraments, it is part of the fabric of human life and yet it points beyond it. Like all the sacraments, it has suffered at times from a one-sided emphasis on its transcendental dimension, to the point of being conceived as radically discontinuous with the other six days of the week. At other times, including our own, its specific Christian identity has been merged with its role as a social institution, a weekly day of recuperation subordinate to the demands of the week's work. In either case, the appreciation of Sunday has been all of a piece with Christians' perception of time itself. To the degree that Christians' concept of the "supernatural" located the life of God in another time and another place, Sunday became a radically different day. To the degree that Christians have adopted the cultural images of time and history, Sunday becomes a merely cultural institution: time off, or time for overtime. To the degree, however, that we understand the Gospel to offer us an alternative vision of the future—and thus to demand an alternative set of present values, an alternative way of living in time—Sunday itself will have a specifically Christian meaning, embodying that vision, proleptic of that future, and gathering to itself those whose loyalties are to that alternative way of living in time.

Thus the importance of Sunday goes far beyond the merely sociological one of how to get our churches filled. It has to do with allowing our culturally compromised understanding of the Gospel itself first to be shattered and then fashioned anew, that we might be faithful to it into the future. The way we live Sunday will then become an experiment in the reconquest of time itself, the "source and summit" of the weekly life cycle of the Christian. Sunday morning, the time of Eucharistic assembly, will lend character to the day as the day will in turn set the tone for the week.

The papers in this collection were first delivered at the Tenth Annual Conference of the Notre Dame Center for Pastoral Liturgy, held at the University of Notre Dame in June 1981. They are offered now to a wider audience in the hope that they might contribute not only to making more of Sunday morning, but to the recovery of a Christian identity and life-style which will give "future generations reasons for living and hoping." They offer a variety of perspectives on this wonderful sacrament we call Sunday, and no attempt has been made to reconcile them. The variety, the overlapping, and even some mutual disagreement should serve to push the mind and the imagination beyond the search for new answers to old questions about how to keep Sunday. For indeed, what is at issue here is not how we may keep Sunday, but how Sunday might keep us.

The Origins of Sunday in the New Testament

EUGENE LAVERDIERE, S.S.S.

Our contemporary search for the origins of Sunday in the New Testament can be compared to history's quests for the sources of the world's great rivers. At first, the undertaking appears quite simple. We are familiar with the deltas and the mighty channels. However, as we make our way upriver, the streams bifurcate and multiply. We wonder whether we have abandoned the main channel. As we finally approach the source or sources, little resembles the mighty river downstream. So it is with Sunday, whose New Testament origins bear little relationship to subsequent history's institutionalized day of rest and worship with its cultural incarnation of Christian religious values.

This essay investigates the sources of Sunday in the New Testament era. The first step is to clear away a number of later developments which are not associated with the beginnings. This preliminary effort should enable us to view the truly distinctive aspects of Sunday more clearly. The second section focuses on the positive characteristics and values

---

EUGENE LAVERDIERE is well known as a lecturer both in this country and abroad. A member of the Congregation of the Blessed Sacrament, he studied Scripture in Rome, Jerusalem, and the University of Chicago. He is presently associate professor of New Testament at the Chicago Theological Union, associate editor of *The Bible Today*, and contributing editor of *Emmanuel*.

of Sunday as it emerged in the first century. This second effort should prepare us to distinguish what is essential from what is nonessential in our contemporary expression of Sunday. The final section develops a New Testament theology of Sunday by comparing and contrasting Sunday and the sabbath. Such a theology should help us to meet the challenges of an increasingly secular world which is gradually eroding the public observance of Sunday as we have known it in much of the world.

I. Clearing the Cultural Field

We begin this study by clearing our cultural field of elements which are now associated with Sunday but which were altogether absent in New Testament times. In doing so, we shall focus on the name Sunday as well as on Sunday's position as a Christian sabbath, a civil day of rest and a public day of worship.

The Name Sunday

The name Sunday, which we now use and which can be found on any western calendar, religious and secular, is of Roman origin. In the Roman week, it was the day of the sun, *dies solis*, a special day which reflected the ascendancy of the imperial cult of the Invincible Sun, *Sol Invictus*.

In the first-century Roman calendar, the day of the sun was the second day of the week. Culturally, it thus corresponded to our Monday. The first day was that of Saturn, from which we derive the name Saturday. The Roman week thus extended from Saturday to Friday, and the day of the sun did not stand out as the first and most important day of the week.

The Jewish and Christian calendars, however, did not coincide with the official Roman calendar. While the Romans were observing the day of Saturn, the first day of their week, both Jews and Jewish Christians were observing the same day as the sabbath, i.e., the seventh and last day of the week. For the Jews, the second day, that of the sun, had no special significance. For the Christians, however, both Jewish and gentile, this second Roman day coincided with the most significant day of the Christian week. Using a name drawn from the Jewish calendar, they referred to it as "the first day of the week" (1 Cor 16:2; Acts 20:7). With regard to their calendars, Jews and Christians of the first century were thus culturally dissonant with the Roman world in which they lived.

The second century saw an important shift in the Roman calendar. With the growing influence of the eastern provinces on Roman political and cultural life, the day of the sun displaced the day of Saturn as the first day of the week. The way was thus open for Christians to adopt the name and give it Christian significance. Baptizing the day of the sun, they celebrated the Sun of Justice and gradually inserted themselves into the Roman world.

While adopting the Roman day of the sun, however, Christians also found it necessary to stress its Christian uniqueness. They thus offset the danger of absorption which accompanied their Roman acculturation. It is at this time that the name Lord's Day (*kuriakē hēmera*), first attested in Revelation 1:10, became increasingly prominent. In the Latin-speaking world, the expression was rendered as *dominicus dies* (Tertullian, *De Oratione* 23 and *De Corona* 3), from which the Romance languages derived the modern names *dimanche*, *domenica*, and *domingo*.

Sunday as a Christian Sabbath

For many centuries, Christians have approached Sunday as a transposed sabbath, uniquely Christian but with all the basic social functions once fulfilled by the Jewish sabbath. Sunday has thus been viewed as a religiously sanctioned civil day of rest and as a public day of worship. This situation is quite different from that of New Testament times, when Jewish Christians continued to observe the sabbath along with the rest of the Jewish world. In gentile Christian communities, when sabbath observance was set aside, it was not replaced by a corresponding Christian sabbath. The New Testament environment, whether Jewish or gentile, simply did not provide the ground for a Christian sabbath to emerge.

We must consequently dissociate Sunday from the observance of a day of rest. For Jewish Christians, the day of rest was the sabbath. The beginning of Sunday coincided with the resumption of normal work rhythms. This can best be appreciated by those who have lived in Israel and watched all work and business cease with the sabbath sundown, only to spark to life with the beginning of Sunday on Saturday evening. The following morning, when all is quiet in the Christian world, Israel's trucks roll out onto the highways. Culturally, for a Christian, it is Monday. So it was in first-century Judaea and Galilee and in the Jewish enclaves of the Greco-Roman cities, where Sunday was the first of six days of work, not a day of rest. For gentile Christian communities, it was merely another workday, the second in a seven-day week.

Nor must we view the origins of Sunday as a public day of worship. For Jewish Christians, the day of worship was the sabbath, a day for studying the Law and for prayer. At first these activities focused on the synagogue. However, as the Law received an increasingly Christian interpretation and prayer became distinctively Christian, there was less and less room for them in the synagogue. They thus turned to the privacy of the Christian home, where reflection on Scripture and prayer became associated with the Lord's Supper. As in the gentile Christian communities, Sunday was the day on which they found time to worship. However, this is quite different from observing Sunday itself as the day institutionally devoted to worship. The Sunday of our Christian origins was consequently much closer to a Catholic Holy Day, which falls during the week and which is celebrated in a country like the United States, than to our modern Sunday.

II. The First Day of the Week

Having cleared our cultural field, we now explore the distinctive elements which constituted Sunday at its origins. For the New Testament Christians, the principal way of referring to Sunday was "the first [day] of the week" (*hē mia tōn sabbatōn*). A survey of New Testament references to it shows that it was the day on which the Christians regularly gathered for an assembly at which they saw to practical matters such as the collection for the poor (1 Cor 16:2), shared the Gospel and participated in their characteristic meal (Acts 20:7-12; Luke 24:13-35). The first day is also associated with the Christian experience of the risen Lord (Mark 16:2; Matt 28:1; Luke 24:1; John 20:1, 19, 26). Three sets of considerations will help us to appreciate its place and significance in early Christian life.

The Name

First we shall examine the expression *the first [day] of the week*. Translations cover the fact that in Greek this expression or name varies in its wording. For the word *first* we usually find the cardinal number *one* (Mark 16:2; Matt 28:1; Luke 24:1; Acts 20:7; John 20:1, 19), but in an early second-century text, we also find the ordinal *first* (Mark 16:9). The word *week* is always the Jewish designation *sabbath*, and its normal form is the plural (Mark 16:2; Matt 28:1; Luke 24:1; Acts 20:7; John 20:1, 19). However, the singular form is also found (1 Cor 16:2; Mark 16:9).

This variety in the form of the expression indicates that, while the first day of the week was significant for the New Testament Christians, its role as an institution which shaped the rhythm of life and gave it consistency was only beginning to emerge. This conclusion is supported by John's reference to "after eight days" instead of to "the next first day of the week" in 20:26 (see also Luke 9:28). A solid and clearly defined institution would have produced a uniformly accepted name for that day.

Use of the term *sabbath* as the designation for week and within the special expression *the first day of the week* also indicates that the expression and the beginnings of Sunday are rooted in early Jewish Christianity and that this practice was firm enough to carry over into gentile Christian contexts without being displaced by a corresponding Greek term.

The plural for sabbath very likely reflects septuagintal influence on New Testament language (Exod 20:10; Deut 5:15). The use of the cardinal *mia* may stem from the same source. Hebrew uses the cardinal number and not the ordinal to express *first* and this was literally translated in the Septuagint's Genesis 1:5, where *first day* is *hēmera mia*. Departures from both of these forms indicates removal from septuagintal and Jewish influence.

Relationship to the Resurrection

The emergence of the first day of the week in the New Testament is inseparable from the early Christian recall of the first visits to the tomb, the Christian understanding which these experiences eventually brought about, and the stories which gradually clothed them with symbolic value and transformed them into vehicles of gospel proclamation, prophecy, and apologetic. The day was also associated with experiences of the risen Lord, experiences in which the disciples first passed out of darkness into light and which characterized the community's ongoing life at every stage of its internal development and expansion.

At its origins and throughout the first century, the first day of the week consequently was not viewed and celebrated as the day of the resurrection itself, but as the day on which Christians experienced the risen Lord. Not until the early second century would it be presented as the day on which Jesus actually rose (Mark 16:9). With this development, the first day of the week came to be viewed more and more as a particular date in the history of Christianity, the first Easter. Indeed it was, but the day's primitive association with experiences of the risen Lord guaranteed that it would also be viewed as a recurrent day in the monthly calendar. As the first century unfolded, the date of Jesus' resurrection gradually receded into the past. The experience of the risen Lord, however, remained ever actual in the weekly celebration of the first day of the week.

These distinctions and conclusions are well supported by the various expressions which gradually displaced the first day of the week as the Christian designation for Sunday in the late New Testament and early patristic period. The most fundamental of these expressions appears in Revelation 1:10, the *Lord's Day* (*hē kyriakē hēmera*). In English and other modern languages, this expression is easily confused with the *Day of the Lord*, (*hē hēmera tou kyriou*), the eschatological day of the Lord's coming. In Greek, however, *Lord* is an adjective (*kyriakos*) and not a substantive (*kyrios*), a clear indication that the day's focus was on the Christian relationship to the risen Lord and not on the risen Lord himself. This sensitivity is also demonstrated by the apocryphal work known as the Gospel of Peter, which twice refers to the Lord's Day with the simple adjectival designation *hē kyriakē*, ("the Lord's"), with no mention of the noun *hēmera* ("day") which it modified (vv. 35, 50). Such a practice is a clear indication of common or at least fairly widespread usage among Christians of the time.

Even when we find greater focus on the risen Lord himself, the experiential aspect remains. The Didache, for example, and the letter of Ignatius of Antioch to the Magnesians (9:1) refer to "the Lord's [day] of the Lord" (*kata kyriakēn de kyriou*), an expression which appears tautological, but only when we disregard the day's twofold relationship. The fact that *the Lord's* was not altogether displaced by *of the Lord* attests to the strength and persistence of the experience of the risen Lord in the early Christian observance of the first day of the week.

Relationship to the Christian Assembly

The special relationship between the first day of the week and the experience of the risen Lord is intimately bound up with the Christian assembly for the Lord's Supper. It is in the Lord's Supper or breaking of bread that the Christians experienced and recognized the risen Lord. The assembly's reflection on its own life and development in light of the Scriptures and of all that Jesus did and said prepared them to meet the risen Lord and find new life. The sharing which characterized their meal opened their eyes to the Lord's presence, bonded them in his fellowship, overflowed into daily life, and propelled them into the mission with a gospel word deeply inscribed in their flesh.

All of these life values are reflected in the New Testament narratives of the resurrection, which situate Jesus' appearances in meals which took place on the first day of the week and relate these meal appearances to the Lord's word, communal sharing, and the Christian mission. We can safely conclude that the significance of the first day of the week stemmed both from the earliest historical experience of the risen Lord and from the Lord's Supper, which allowed later generations to join in that experience. Its weekly celebration assured growth in both depth and scope as the Church assumed the challenges of history in the rapidly expanding world of Christian origins.

While appreciating the extraordinary significance of the first day of the week, however, we must not assume that the day had acquired institutional value comparable to our

Sunday. As we noted earlier, variance in the Greek form of the day's name counters such an assumption. Further evidence comes from the particular time of day when the assembly gathered.

In Acts 20:7-12, which speaks of a particular assembly at Troas on the first day of the week, Luke also mentions the following day (*epaurion*), when Paul is to leave. The assembly took place in the evening of the first day and extended until Paul's departure at dawn of the second day of the week. Again in Luke 24:13-35 and 36-49, the breaking of bread at Emmaus and the assembly in Jerusalem both occur during the evening of the first day of the week. In each of these instances, Luke is consequently not following the Jewish calendar, which closed the sabbath and ended at the following sundown. With this calendar, the assembly would have taken place not on the first day but at the beginning of the second. The Lukan day extended rather from dawn to dawn. The time of the celebration thus corresponded to our Sunday evening, and in exceptional circumstances (Acts 20:7-12) it could extend into the early hours of our Monday.

As in Luke and Acts, the two assemblies in John 20:19-25 and 26-29 also occur on the evening of the first day of the week. However, the appearance to Mary Magdalene (John 20:11-18) took place much earlier in the day, which began with her visit to the tomb early in the morning of the first day of the week (John 20:1-2). Mark and Matthew also situated the resurrection experience early in the morning of the first day of the week (Matt 28:1; Mark 16:2).

In summary, then, for the New Testament Christians, the first day of the week was extremely significant, but not as a religious institution in a sociological sense. It was clearly related to the resurrection and the Christian assembly for the Lord's Supper. However, it would be anachronistic to think of it as the day of the resurrection or the day of the assembly. Emphasis was rather on the Christian experience of the risen Lord, an experience which was shared in the assembly. The first day of the week was the day on which the Christians assembled, experienced the risen Lord, recognized his presence in the unexpected, and opened themselves to one another and to others in the Lord's fellowship.

The New Testament thus cautions us against approaching Sunday with a focus on the resurrection, on the risen Lord, or on the assembly as independent and absolute values. Apart from the assembly's experience of the risen Lord, such a Sunday would have held little transforming power for Christian life. Perhaps our investigation has uncovered one of the sources for the current malaise concerning Sunday.

III. SUNDAY AND THE SABBATH

Although Sunday did not originate as a Christian extension or transposition of the Jewish sabbath, it did eventually develop into an institution patterned on the sabbath. This development, whose remote origins coincided with the Church's quest for social acceptance in the second century, climaxed in Christianity's establishment as an imperial religion in the fourth century. Now that the new social and political order included the Church, Christians turned afresh to the Old Testament in search of models to formulate relationships of Church and State. The Israelite monarchy enabled them to distinguish and integrate the various roles and institutions into one harmonious whole. In this context, Sunday was presented as the Christian sabbath, a social institution of religious as well as political significance. Such is the general form of Sunday as it has persisted to the present in the western world, where it is now undergoing considerable change as a result of growing secularization.

In this final section of my presentation, I shall address the relationship between Sunday and the sabbath. My purpose is to develop a New Testament theology of Sunday which recognizes its long traditional relationship to the sabbath as well as the social changes now taking place. In doing so, I shall first explore the biblical significance and purpose of the sabbath. Second, I shall examine Jesus' relationship to the sabbath and how he saw its fulfillment. Third, I shall show how, from a New Testament point of view, although Sunday is related to the sabbath, it is essentially distinct and uniquely Christian.

The Sabbath

For Israel, first-century Judaism, and New Testament Christianity, the sabbath was a day which the Lord had blessed and made holy. It was associated first of all with the work of creation. For six days, God had worked—from the command that there be light to the creation of the human couple in his image and likeness (Gen 1:1-31). When all was complete, he crowned his work on the seventh day with a blessed and holy day of rest (Gen 2:1-3).

The sabbath was also associated with the Lord God's historic liberation of Israel from Egypt. Freed from bondage (Exod 20:2; Deut 5:6), Israel would remember the sabbath day. Sharing in God's own freedom, Israel would rest on the Lord's sabbath, observing it as a blessed and holy day (Exod 20:8-11; Deut 5:12-15).

The sabbath was consequently a celebration of both creation and liberation, and its ultimate grounding lay in God's role as creator and Lord of history. Like their creator, the Israelites would observe the sabbath as a day of rest. They would do so in the awareness that God himself had made them a free people.

The sabbath, however, was not only a celebration of God's creative and liberating action in the past. It was also a commitment to Israel's role in the work of creation and to Israel's ongoing liberation. The weekly observance of the sabbath strengthened Israel's self-awareness as co-creator, assured that she would not look back to the security of bondage, and guaranteed that she would resist every foreign effort to enslave her.

The sabbath also had implications for Israel's relationship to other peoples. In her freedom, Israel would not enslave other human beings, all of whom were created by a God who rested on the seventh day. Like Israel—and Israel's children—all of living creation which was associated with Israel would thus share in God's freedom and observe the sabbath as a day of rest. In its weekly celebration, the sabbath thus guaranteed Israel's own freedom and committed Israel to the freedom of others.

Such were the implications of God's command that Israel remember the sabbath day (Exod 20:8). The sabbath was a memorial in the full sense of the term, a celebration of creation and of Israel's liberation, a grateful expression of Israel's goodness and dignity as a free creature, and a commitment to the work of co-creation and of liberation for all. By observing the sabbath, Israel acknowledged her place in creation and accepted her role as co-creator with God. She also recognized her place in history as a liberated people, committed to be God's co-liberator on behalf of all peoples.

Jesus and the Sabbath

In Jesus' time, the sabbath in itself retained all of its Old Testament meaning, and it is as such that Jesus celebrated it in fulfillment of the Law. Concretely, however, many of the Jews had moved away from some of the sabbath's most basic values. Under Roman occupation, they had largely forgotten their commitment to the liberation of others. The sabbath thus celebrated the life of a people besieged and struggling for survival. Severed from its outreach and cut off from its ultimate grounding in universal creation, this ghetto sabbath had become stultified, an institution to be maintained for its own sake, with little or no regard for its purpose. Jesus' celebration of the sabbath was consequently bound to assume a prophetic quality.

The Gospels frequently present Jesus as a prophetic figure calling his fellow Jews to a genuine sabbath observance. In Luke 4:16-30, for example, we find Jesus going to synagogue on the sabbath as he regularly did. His message, drawn from Isaiah, proclaims his own mission and commitment to bring good news to the poor, to announce liberation to captives, to extend sight to the blind and freedom to prisoners. The sabbath is a weekly sign of the sabbatical year of jubilee (Luke 4:18-19). His own commitment must be shared by all who join him in solidarity for the sabbath observance. The synagogue of Nazareth, however, is unable to accept this role, which was too firmly rooted in Israel's most ancient prophetic tradition (Luke 4:23-30). Refusing to reach out to others, the synagogue rejects its own liberation and frustrates the very purpose of sabbath celebration.

On another occasion, when the disciples were plucking grain, shelling it, and eating it on the sabbath, Jesus was forced to recall the purpose of the sabbath. Evoking an incident in David's story, he showed the Pharisees how the sabbath observance is governed by greater values. He was in their midst as the Son of Man, reminding them as *the* human being that he was Lord of the sabbath (Mark 2:23-28; Matt 12:1-8; Luke 6:1-5). On other sabbaths, he insisted that the entire meaning of the sabbath was distorted when Jews forgot that it was intended to give and preserve life, not to destroy it (Mark 3:1-7; Matt 12:9-15; Luke 6:6-11). Surely it was lawful to cure on the sabbath (Luke 14:1-6). By refusing to give life, the Pharisees lost it for themselves. What purpose, then, their sabbath observance?

For a people that had been emancipated but that needed to appropriate and share its freedom, the sabbath was a promise. In his sabbath observance, Jesus fulfilled that promise. He did so as *the* human being, revealing the fullness of God's human creation in his image and likeness. Risen, he would also do so as Lord of all, manifesting God's liberating lordship in history. Thus it was that he called his fellow Jews and all human beings to the sabbath's divine intention for them: "The sabbath was made for man, not man for the sabbath" (Mark 2:27).

Sunday

The many gospel stories in which Jesus responds to various problems affecting sabbath observance constitute a twofold message. As historical statements, they record events in Jesus' life. As pastoral statements, they also address problems current in the early Christian communities. As such, they provide an important witness to the enduring role of the sabbath in emergent Christianity.

These same Gospels clearly distinguish Sunday, the first day of the week, from the sabbath, which was the seventh and last day of the week. The distinction is most explicit in the synoptic Gospels, which indicate that the sabbath was over (Mark 16:1; Matt 28:1) or that it was observed as a day of rest according to the law (Luke 23:56) before moving on to the events of the first day of the week (Mark 16:2; Matt 28:1; Luke 24:1). They thus invite us to investigate the special meaning of Sunday in Christian life.

In some ways, the significance of Sunday is quite similar to that of the sabbath. Its relationship to the resurrection parallels the sabbath's relationship to both creation and liberation. The early Christians saw Jesus' resurrection as a new creation, an event which responded to Jesus' life and death in the old creation but which was radically new. They also saw Jesus' resurrection as a salvific event, freeing all human beings from the historical bonds which defined their human associations too narrowly and prevented them from realizing the fulfillment to which they were called. This dual relationship was concretely and experientially realized through the early Christian sharing in the Lord's Supper, for which they gathered on Sunday, the first day of the week.

Sunday's similarity to the sabbath, however, must not obscure its uniqueness. The most important indication of this uniqueness lies in the very name *first day of the week*. Our reflections must consequently focus on the difference between celebrating the first day as opposed to the last day of the week.

The sabbath constituted a climax in the work of creation and liberation. It looked primarily to the past, to the work which God had completed and to what his human creatures had already accomplished as co-creators. Its observance thus reminded the Jewish people and the early Christians of the goodness and blessedness of the world about them. As a day of rest, it called them to accept their freedom and to recognize their obligation to respect it in the future, both for themselves and for others.

Sunday, however, was not a climax but a radical new beginning. Unlike the sabbath, its primary stance was not with regard to the past but to the future. Sunday was consequently not a day of rest but a day of work. Such were the implications of celebrating not Jesus' resurrection in itself, an event which stood in the past, but the Christian experience of the risen Lord, an event which marked the present and associated Christians with the risen Lord in the gradual unfolding of the new creation and the ongoing liberation of humanity. The single most important term to designate this work was the *kingdom of God*, a reality already in the midst of the Christian communities and to whose full manifestation they committed their lives and energies. The celebration of the breaking of the bread on the first day of the week was thus intimately related to the Christian mission, to the primary work of evangelization, whose ultimate horizons were eschatologically defined by the kingdom of God.

The Christian attitudes which govern Sunday are thus

related to the first day of creation rather than to the seventh. Christians are called upon over and over again to recognize the light which God brings into the chaos, the disorder and darkness all about them. On the first day of the week, they experience the personal light of the world and accept their mission to join the risen Lord in manifesting the light by holding it aloft. They commit themselves as the risen Lord's historical agents in establishing the new order of creation and giving birth to a new humanity.

On the first day of the week, Christians also engage themselves in the Passover. In doing so, however, they do not so much look back to how God has liberated them as to how in the midst of slavery he calls them to liberation and to liberating others. In the Eucharist, they thus see themselves in Egypt rather than in the promised land. In their experience of the risen Lord in the breaking of bread, they stand poised on the edge of the Passover journey as Jesus had done at the Last Supper, open to joining him in his self-offering as the lamb of sacrifice. Like him, they would find liberation and life by offering their lives for others.

In the Sunday assembly, the early Christians thus did what Jesus had done, themselves becoming the human manifestations of the risen Lord in history. They thus proclaimed the death of the Lord until his coming (1 Cor 11:26), and they renewed their baptismal commitment to die and to be buried with him that they might live with him and ultimately rise with him.

The fundamental challenge for renewing our Sunday celebration is consequently quite clear. There are good grounds for maintaining Sunday's relationship to the sabbath. However, as we appropriate the sabbath and its religious values into our observance of Sunday, we must respect the uniqueness of Sunday. In the course of history, we may have unwittingly allowed Sunday to be absorbed by the sabbath. It is rather the sabbath which must be absorbed by and transformed into Sunday. Close attention to this distinction will enable us to transcend the various crises now affecting Sunday observance and will guide us in our rediscovery of Sunday as the first day of the week.

Suggested Reading

Bacchiocchi, Samuele. *From Sabbath to Sunday, a Historical Investigation of the Rise of Sunday Observance in Early Christianity.* Rome: The Pontifical Gregorian University Press, 1977.

Grelot, Pierre. "Du sabbat juif au dimanche chrétien," *La Maison-Dieu* (1975) 123:79–107; 124:14–54.

Rordorf, W. *The History of the Day of Rest and Worship in the Earliest Centuries of the Christian Church.* Philadelphia: Westminster Press, 1968.

——————— . *Sabbat et dimanche dans l'Eglise ancienne.* Neuchatel: Delachaux et Niestlé Editeurs, 1972.

Sunday Assembly in the Tradition

ROBERT W. HOVDA

Interpreting the title of this session broadly, I plan to isolate what seem to be commonly accepted elements of the Sunday assembly tradition and, on the basis of these elements, raise certain questions regarding our present practice. Our own time and our own Church life are also part of a living tradition. And the questions posed by our recently and vastly improved understanding of biblical literature and of the earliest period of Church history are the urgent questions for us, particularly in view of the reformation character of the contemporary Church era.

Some of those questions are extremely uncomfortable, but honesty with respect to both our own experience and the sources and roots recently revealed to us requires our dealing with them. It will be evident that the questions come from an honest attempt to be open to the meaning of the Sunday assembly in the tradition. Any answers proposed are offered for critical examination, although I certainly am not alone in suggesting them. In a reformation time like ours, there is at least some recognition that the rediscovery and

---

ROBERT HOVDA, a priest of the diocese of Fargo, North Dakota, has for many years been in the forefront of liturgical renewal in the United States. He has been closely associated with the work of the Liturgical Conference, where he has been an outstanding spokesman for ecumenism and social justice. He is currently working in parish ministry at St. Joseph's Church in Greenwich Village.

vitality we seek depend on some sorting out of customs and
some shucking of attachments. Some discomfort is caused
by the venerable age of those customs and attachments. They
are powerful, and they account for the extremely visible
emergence of a counterreformation even before our conciliar
reformation draws its second breath. It is difficult enough
to get us to shuck a bad habit for the sake of a good one. It
is even more difficult to get us to shuck what seem to be good
habits for the sake of better ones. And the latter is often what
the questions I refer to seem to require.

I. ELEMENTS OF THE TRADITION

Something must first be said about the relationship between
Judaism and Christianity, however, because it is basic to an
appreciation of these questions. If we accept the still-popular
notion of the discontinuity—even opposition—between
Judaism and Christianity, we prejudice our grasp of both the
Sunday assembly and the tradition. At least on a sophisticated
level of our membership, we Christians are finally beginning
to regain some sense of our own Jewishness, of our depend-
ence on and our intimate relation with Judaism (not only
Judaism before Jesus, but the Judaism that continues to exist
as a twin covenant community with ourselves). We have
learned that the Church could well have remained a movement within Judaism, had there not been a fairly general
expulsion of Christian communities from synagogue life
and worship in the latter part of the first century A.D. In his
study of early Christian worship, Ferdinand Hahn writes:
"Official separation between Judaism and Christianity did
not take place until the end of the first century, and was in-
stigated primarily by Judaism, not by Christianity."[1]

---

1. Ferdinand Hahn, *The Worship of the Early Church* (Philadelphia: Fortress
Press, 1973) 33.

We are beginning to be suspicious of those easy contrasts between Judaism and Christianity which we have been in the habit of drawing during almost two millennia of exaggeration, conflict, and tragic persecution. We know now how weak their foundations are. We admit that we have spoken habitually of the "old" and the "new" covenants in a fashion much too glib and self-assured. Covenant, we are learning again, is one mysterious reality, needing periodic renewal. The easy contrast between "letter" and "spirit" is a false and totally misleading way of distinguishing between Judaism and Christianity. It accurately describes a tension in both, but it is a tension which was part of Jewish faith-life before Jesus, just as it remains part of both Jewish and Christian faith-life after Jesus.

We all have favorite theologians. One of mine is Joseph Sittler of Chicago. About these contrasts he writes:

> I am convinced that we . . . end up with what is not only a dichotomy but an opposition between law and gospel because we misread the Old Testament radically. . . . I would think a good exercise would be to start with the Psalms and open yourself without any sophistication and ask, "What kind of language does the Psalmist use when he talks about the law?" "O, how I love thy law. It is a river of ever-renewed freshness. It is a fountain of living water. I meditate upon thy law day and night." Does this sound like a code of ethics or a coercive guide telling you what to eat, what to drink, how far you can go? This beautiful, lyrical, affectionate, holy language about the law should suggest to the mind that even the four gospels do not talk about the law that way because they are reporting the teaching of Jesus over against a Sadducean and a Pharisaical pedagogizing of the law, making it absolute instructions of a catechetical kind. Now, confound it, if only we would let the Old Testament speak to us about the law in its own way! "O, how I love thy law, I meditate on it day and night. It is like bathing in a fresh river or finding water in the middle of a desert: cool, running water." By Torah the Old Testament means the infinite loving kindness of God; . . . Torah tells of the loving kindness, the patience, the covenant-making faith-

fulness which can be counted upon. . . . The word "law" is simply a lousy translation for Torah. If the English word "law" meant the structure of all things as God intends them, then we would have something close to Torah.[2]

The sorting that a time of renewal requires is in no way a rejection of the Christian belief in the Spirit-guidance of tradition. Just the opposite: it is that belief that demands both the sorting and the shucking. One of the aphorisms of Henri de Lubac which I remember from my youth is: "So that the river of tradition may come down to us, we must continually dredge its bed." Whatever we call it, it tries to be faithful to that delicate growth of obedience to God's word and continuity with the believing Church of other times and places. It recognizes, however, that we live in a very untidy world and that all kinds of influences—some of them inimical to the good news, others merely irrelevant—creep into the life of the Church and attach themselves to the organic growth in one way or another. So we get tumors and camouflage and dangling appendices galore. To resort to another figure, we get detours and blind alleys and dead-end streets. And one must have a strong faith community at hand, jealous of its biblical and liturgical formation, if one is going to be able to discern and sort. Our faith is not that foreign elements do not creep into the practice of the Church, but that they will be, must be, sifted out in time.

Biblical faith communities, whether Jewish or Christian, are communities of seekers, always unfinished, incomplete, pilgrim, growing, changing. We do not spring full-grown from some initial acceptance of the covenant, but rather put ourselves in the hands of a God who is still creating, inviting, and drawing us toward that fulfillment which we call God's reign. Our progress is complicated by these influences and

2. Joseph Sittler, "Law and Gospel," *The Grace Note* (Chicago: Augustana Lutheran Church of Hyde Park, September 1980) 2.

pressures. Writing about the sabbath, von Allmen quotes J. J. Stamm:

> . . . the history of the Sabbath in Israel . . . is the history of an ever-deepening consciousness of meaning: at first, the social bearing of the Sabbath is recognized; and later, its implications for the saving process and for the cosmos as a whole are understood.[3]

Applying the same insight into the transitory nature of the faith community as a growing, developing organism, the liturgical pioneer and visionary H. A. Reinhold said the following about "The Christian Meaning of Sunday" in a Liturgical Week address way back in 1949:

> The minerals of the ground that nourished and fed the seed of Sunday are the periodicity of rest and worship in the Old Testament, the Sabbath, the same occurrences in the pagan religions and secular societies surrounding the young church, the facts of human nature, the organizing laws of councils like Nicaea, the Lateran and Trent, and of emperors, kings and rulers like Constantine, Charlemagne, and the sovereigns and parliaments of states.[4]

With all of these relevant and irrelevant influences coming to bear upon the one developing practice in a growing Church, it is easy to see why sorting is necessary if one is concerned about the question: What is really and authentically of the tradition?

There are so many different current interpretations of the slim data we possess about the beginnings of Sunday assembly that one hesitates to affirm anything without reservation. We know that at least some Christian communities continued to observe the Sabbath even after the official separation from Judaism—some for generations, some perhaps

---

3. J.-J. von Allmen, *Worship: Its Theology and Practice* (New York: Oxford University Press, 1965) 214.

4. H. A. Reinhold, *Sanctification of Sunday: National Liturgical Week Proceedings* (Conception, Mo.: The Liturgical Conference, 1949) 64.

for centuries. A recent study explains the persistence of Sabbath observance among Christians:

> Primitive Christians understood Jesus' attitude toward the Sabbath not as a veiled forecast of a new day of worship, but as a perspective of Sabbath-keeping. This consisted both in a new meaning and in a new manner of observance of the Sabbath.[5]

So, whether the Christian assembly was in the earliest period an additional gathering after the observance of the sabbath or a gathering that gradually eclipsed the sabbath observance, it is clear that the sabbath remained the sabbath. Whatever the first day meant for this or that Christian community, it was in *no* case a transplanted sabbath. It seems more likely that the first day was not treated as a special day at all, apart from the gathering, until later. Some say Constantine initiated the movement in this direction, prompted by a polemical attitude toward the Jews as well as by the prominence of the sun cult. And even though the Sunday assembly became established custom early in the Church's life, any linking of the first day with the resurrection appears to have been a much later development, not common until the fourth and fifth centuries.

There is general agreement, however, about a common spirit that informed the variety of early practice. Among all the followers of the way of Jesus, there was a great feeling of fulfillment, a conviction that a new age had dawned, that they were living in a new time. Even for Aramaic-speaking Jewish Christians who remained closely identified with synagogue life, the message of Jesus had successfully communicated a tremendous freedom with respect to "religious practices." Hahn describes their attitude: "What is crucial for

---

5. Samuele Bacchiocchi, *From Sabbath to Sunday: A Historical Investigation of the Rise of Sunday Observance in Early Christianity* (Rome: The Pontifical Gregorian University Press, 1977) 72.

Jesus is not what God has done and required in the past, but his eschatological action in the present. He therefore proclaimed the irruption of God's eschatological rule."[6] That conviction, while it did not diminish reverence for the Bible and tradition, promoted a liberty with respect to forms which accounts for the confusion and variety of worship practices among the early Christians. There could not be a "sacred-profane" dichotomy, or even distinction, in this new creation. What the prophets had strained for and proposed as an ideal was not, in the Messianic Age, the actual world of the believer. All places, all days, and all work belong to God in a quite new sense. The preparation for all this was over, the eschaton had dawned, the realization was here. One can see why there was so little interest—even among those gentile churches that were least attached to the sabbath—in identifying any particular day or any particular place with God's reign. The Lord's way had been prepared. Special places and special days were part of that preparation. In the first flush of that eschatological consciousness, it would have been surprising if any attention had been paid to the cultural means for their survival.

While days and places may have been regarded as of little consequence by the followers of the new Way, the assembly was important and essential from the beginning. Hahn mentions the one exception to the general novelty of the language employed in worship by the first generations of the Church:

> Almost none of the traditional concepts occur in the New Testament; and where they do, they are unmistakably used metaphorically. Cultic terminology is consciously avoided for Christian worship; it serves only to characterize the temple worship of the Old Testament, and to describe the Christ-event or the conduct of Christians in the world. The only term that occurs with a certain regularity is *synerchesthai* ("come together") or *synagesthai* ("to be gathered together"). The

6. Hahn, *The Worship of the Early Church* 13.

"coming together" of the faithful is the significant feature of
Christian worship; and where the community comes together,
God is praised, his mighty acts are proclaimed, prayers are
said, and the Lord's Supper is celebrated.[7]

Among divergent studies and varieties of interpretation of
that period, there seems to be general agreement on that
coming together, that *assembly*, as being the primary, the
most primitive and basic characteristic of Christian worship
in our tradition. There seems to be further agreement that
the gathering is related to the disciples' sense of collective
mission in the world, their sense that their community reality
is to be a sign of a new age. And there seems to be still further
agreement that they come together to celebrate the *Eucharist*,
at first as an eschatological banquet *with* the Lord and a little
later also as a memorial *of* the Lord's death.

These three elements—assembly, mission, Eucharist—
are constant in our tradition, sometimes eclipsed or shadowed
by other realities, but never repudiated. Every serious effort
at Church reform and renewal, including our own beginnings
of a magnificent conciliar reform, is in some way aimed at the
recovery of these elements and at their reestablishment in
true priority. Therefore, it is imperative to raise certain
questions regarding the correspondence between these elements and our present practice.

II. QUESTIONS FOR PRESENT PRACTICE

1. *Assembly*

What questions does that first item of consensus raise: the
gathering, the assembly? In our experience of Christian life
today, is it evident that the primary mark and characteristic
and justification and meaning of the Sunday assembly is

7. *Ibid.* 35–36.

precisely that—the assembly, the gathering, the being-called-together of all the sisters and brothers of the local church? "Not at all," we have to say. And is this not a problem?

Throughout the history of the tradition, as well as now, other "values" have threatened that primacy of the assembly, and many of them are still very much with us. Just look around on Sunday. Many of the problems are as obvious in small parishes as in large ones: is there a celebration that really tries to bring all of us together, or are there multiple celebrations—to accommodate the crowd, to occupy the available clergy, to suit our private preferences? do the people gathered seem to know each other and share a common sense of purpose in life? do they try to sit together and act like participants? Some of the problems are more evident in large parishes: how many people make up a gathering? is there a size beyond which a gathering ceases to be a meeting of persons and becomes an anonymous crowd?

The Second Vatican Council has called us to restore the primacy of the gathering, the central importance of the local church, the communal nature of sacraments, initiation, participation, and a sense of being part of the action. We know the rhetoric by heart, but it seems to have no effect on our habits. Impartially, we both implement the Council's vision and retain the contradictory custom. We have met the enemy and it is we.

When Jesus said, "Where two or three are gathered," he abrogated the synagogue requirement of a minimum of ten persons for common prayer. But the crowding of people together in groups so large that no one is missed when absent, so large that urban anonymity rather than mutual support is its mark, so large that involvement and participation become challenges to one's ingenuity rather than ordinary expectations—that kind of supersized Sunday assembly is incongruous with any reasonable traditional description of what it is called to be and to do.

South of the border, the development of base communities is one answer which eventually, no doubt, will have some influence on us too. Here at home, we have widely scattered efforts to divide large parishes into geographical or other units in which human relationships can be experienced. In architecture and the other arts, Debuyst and other leaders recommend the creation of worship spaces for groups of five hundred or thereabouts. Meanwhile, most of our problems with the assembly continue, as we are engaged (presumably) in various attempts to realize the renewed local church in circumstances that condemn those attempts to futility.

The multiplication of Masses on Sunday is a beautiful example of how necessity is the mother of corruption. Somewhere along the line in the local church we had to ask for a second Eucharistic celebration because the growing number of Christians had made our worship space inadequate, and for some reason another local church could not be organized at that moment. This reluctant concession to necessity, once established, promptly forgot its origins, asserted itself as the norm, and, with a number of other developments that tended to minimize the corporate, collective, community-centered nature of the parish and to transform it into a clergy-centered service station for private individuals, left us with the liturgical bedlam Sunday now is in most of our parishes, large and small. I am working now in a small parish that needs probably two Sunday celebrations but boasts five. And that parish has been working at renewal harder than most.

How do we begin to assert seriously the primacy of the gathering in these circumstances, especially when we have so conned ourselves that we really imagine we are performing a pastoral service with these counterproductive round-the-clock celebrations? If we want to do something about this multiplication of Masses, we can, and we will. But we have to want to. And whether we want to is a big question. Countless other questions occur when we begin to concentrate on the primacy of the assembly, but these are enough for now.

2. Mission

The second element that raises questions for us is the agreement among the experts that the gathering is related to the Christians' sense of mission in the world. The question is: how can people who seem to have lost that sense of mission in the world, that sense of being part of a movement that has good news for the world—how can people without this collective spirit really gather and really celebrate in any kind of community way on Sunday? The answer is simple: we can't.

There are many efforts afoot always, and even more since the Council, to try to convert us Christians from acting like consumers, clients, or passive spectators into agents and actors and doers and ministers—to help us *feel* that we are part of a collective ministry and mission. This feeling has to catch hold before there are going to be any sparks in the Sunday assembly. Sparks are there whenever the congregation that gathers has a profound sense of having come from a collective mission in their part of the world, and of having that struggle, that sacrifice, that self-giving, to celebrate and bless and offer. But that is a rare experience.

We tend to expect the assembly to make a community out of us, and we come to the assembly as private individuals. The Church has reality for most of us only in the assembly. That's one of the reasons we have become accustomed, if we are serious about the life of faith, to "coming to church" (as we say) so often. God, Christ, our oneness as the body of Christ and as agents of the new age—these are absent everywhere else. I have to "go to church" to find them. But that is not what the Sunday assembly is for. I have no sense, no feeling, no comprehension that the work I do for a living, my life in the larger community—my political, economic, cultural activity—are my part in our collective mission and ministry. If they are the way I herald the new age and pursue the reign of God, then it's a well-kept secret, from me as well as everybody else.

Alexander Schmemann, an Orthodox theologian, has something to say to those Christians who see this problem but think that the answer is to label tradition and liturgy passé and move "beyond" them:

> Not only the average Christian, even the theologian seems to say: the world of Christian "symbolism" is no longer our world, all this failed, all this is gone. . . . [At] this point let us ask a few questions: Are these "symbols" merely "symbolic"? Or is their failure perhaps to be explained precisely by the symbolic value attached to them by Christians themselves, who ceased to understand their true nature? And did they not cease to understand this nature because at one time . . . Christians came to think that "religion" has nothing to do with time, is in fact salvation from time? Before we gain the right to dispose of the old "symbols" we must understand that the real tragedy of Christianity is not its "compromise" with the world and progressive "materialism," but on the contrary, its "spiritualization" and transformation into "religion."[8]

We Westerners hardly expect to hear that from a theologian of the East, of the Orthodox Church, which we regard as mystical and other-worldly in the extreme! Do we hear what Schmemann is saying? It is critically important for our subject here. Isn't it precisely what we saw earlier as one of the marks of the primitive Christian consciousness—the excitement of fulfillment for all the good and true and beautiful (but limited) ways of old in Jesus' inauguration of the reign of God, in Jesus' presence as the sign that that reign is here and now claiming the whole lives of believers? No longer is the arena of the life of faith some kind of sacred precinct; it is now the world. Institutions, structures, patterns, ways, and customs have to be shaped by the peace and justice, the freedom and oneness, that we possess in Christ, not for ourselves but as God's gift to all the world.

8. Alexander Schmemann, *For the Life of the World* (National Student Christian Federation, 1963) 32.

James García says the same thing another way:

> Frequently this meeting for worship [Sunday assembly] is not founded upon any real community life. . . . Rather, it is the community's life, developing and dynamic, which calls forth and gives meaning to its specifically cultic acts. . . . No wonder that some communities have nothing to celebrate on Sunday. They have lived nothing as a group during the week.[9]

Commenting on some current responses to the old canon law of Sunday "obligation," Christopher Kiesling writes:

> . . . what is really important [re the Sunday assembly] is that the Christian community celebrate its origin, existence and destiny and thereby build itself up. In other words, it is not primarily the individual Christian's fulfillment of a personal responsibility to worship God that is at stake in regard to Sunday worship, but the responsibility of the Christian community to grow.[10]

For the reasons we are discussing at this point, we might be just a little suspicious and perhaps nervous when we hear the word "spirituality" several times each day and see it tacked on to every title that seeks to draw a crowd. May it not be another manifestation, at least subconsciously, of our persistent sin of refusing to challenge with faith's vision the status quo, the demonic powers of the world, refusing to put our lives, our jobs, our homes, our money in the jeopardy required of us by the God who is known in the command to do justice?

The Christian life is ordinarily lived in the middle of the world. The Sunday assembly and the parish refresh the Christian for that work, that world. Full- or part-time ministers in the parish must be very careful that they do not seek to construct a parish life and a schedule of parish activities

---

9. James García, "Contributions and Challenges to the Theology of Sunday," *Worship* 52, no. 4 (July 1978) 373.

10. Christopher Kiesling, *The Future of the Christian Sunday* (New York: Sheed and Ward, 1970) 33.

that will totally consume the time and energy of members of the local church. The job of those members is elsewhere, and the parish is not supposed to exhaust their lives and strength; it is supposed to refresh them and express them. Its claims in time and energy are, therefore, modest.

The question here is another serious one. How do we capture a sense of being a collective movement to change the face of the earth, to proclaim a reign of God? How do we make the connections between how we earn our daily bread and spend it, how we vote, how we relate to the structures and institutions of the status quo—how do we make the connections between these things and our sense of being Church, our mission and ministry? Only when those connections are strong and vital can the Sunday assembly be the experience it is meant to be. We can't really do anything *together* inside the church if we do not feel that we have been doing a marvelously necessary work *together* during the preceding week. That is one of the reasons why the Sunday assembly of a community that knows it is oppressed and knows what it is struggling for is such a tingling and moving experience.

3. Eucharist

The third element of our tradition that raises questions for us is the agreement that from the earliest times the Sunday gathering involved the celebration of the Lord's Supper. At first, it was in the context of an evening meal, a full meal at night; later, it was in an extended liturgical context, but still a table gathering. We sit at table with the Lord at an eschatological banquet, the banquet of a new age, creating the scene of faith's vision, the reign of God, where all are free and all are one, anticipating the object or goal of our mission, thanking God for all we are and have and hope for.

Soon the tradition added to that refreshing meal of the new community with its Head the other aspect of Eucharist —a memorial of the Lord's death. Even in these first stages of our conciliar reform, we have made considerable progress in our understanding of the Eucharist, in opening up its symbolic action, in celebrating it as an assembly rather than merely as a presbyter, in utilizing music and the other arts, in employing a variety of specialized ministries in addition to that basic ministry of the assembly as a whole, and in countless other ways. There are ample opportunities in our Church life, fortunately, for discussion of the many questions that arise from a study of Sunday Eucharistic tradition.

To conclude as briefly as possible, I want to reflect here on just two of those questions, which it seems to me are significantly related. Gerard Sloyan once said, "Economics is a primary theological datum." We like to forget that.

One question has to do with the offering of money with a request for the "intention" of the presiding minister in a Eucharistic celebration. I had hoped that when the general intercessions were restored as an ordinary part of the Eucharist, we might have realized that the intercessions are not only part of our reflection on the word of God but also the presentation of the intentions of our celebration. But in this, as in most other areas of reform, we have shown a remarkable capacity for paradox and contradiction. We do something that indicates a gospel insight and a step forward, and we also carry along a habit that neutralizes our apparent progress.

I do not wish to dwell on this practice of Mass stipends, or to define it in one of the many ways it has been described: as simony, as economic necessity, as a pious and touching devotion of the faithful, or as all three. My problem with it in this connection is that it vitiates on the powerful level of practice the kind of growth in understanding of the Eucharist which I have just mentioned. Money is a powerful symbol. We can preach for years and we will not undo the mindset about Mass which this *quid-pro-quo* bartering and commercial atmosphere induces. Only an abolition of the practice will suffice. If we want to find more suitable means for the support of our ministers, we will.

The other (and related) question is that of daily Eucharistic celebration. The emotional attachment of many Catholics, young and old, to this centuries-old practice, habit, and even environment of the church goes without saying. What is very clear in such a practice is also true, if less clear, in connection with every other practice of piety in a community undergoing a long-overdue reformation and renewal. That is, that to be new persons in Christ Jesus, we have to be willing at all times (not just in our own good time), and every day, to step outside our habits, even those that seem most sacred, in order to see how they affect our relation to Almighty God. Good habits will never yield to better ones unless we are sufficiently unattached and sufficiently free to engage in such dispassionate examination.

We are in the process of trying to regain a Sunday celebration of the Eucharist that is first of all a gathering and expression of the local church, one which brings together not only the members of the body and the work of the week but also all of the gifts and talents, the music and other arts, the preparation and reflection of the community, in an offering of praise. In that process, gradually and increasingly it has become more evident that this is what the Eucharist, as the central sacrament of the Church, is meant to be. Not simply a means of prayer—we have many means of common prayer in our tradition. Not simply a routine discipline by which we turn ourselves toward God in a particularly intentional way—again we have many such means in our tradition. Certainly not in any sense a private or semi-private act.

The adjectives that come to mind as we pursue the goal of an experiential Sunday celebration are "climactic," "celebratory," "communal," "festal," and the like. Traditional forms of common prayer which supply other needs of the faith community, such as daily common prayer, small-group common prayer, etc., are, it would seem, more appropriately the Liturgy of the Hours, particularly its parochial forms of morning and evening prayer or some adaptation thereof.

If every day is a holiday or a feast, then in fact there is, in the experience of people, no holiday or feast at all. If Eucharistic celebration appropriately requires the kind of communal gathering of believers, the kind of previous investment of life and work, the kind of preparation, the kind of incarnation in the arts and talents of the community, even the kind of choreography and logistics that we are again beginning to recognize as belonging to this symbolic action, then the practice of daily Eucharistic celebration presents problems. Whatever the virtues of its theory or practice on a private and individual level, it militates against the Sunday celebration that we are finally seeking.

In the article cited earlier, James García asks:

> Does the weekday Eucharist, through subtle competition, jeopardize Sunday's proper eschatological tension? The Roman Catholic tradition has maintained daily mass, and since the 1600s it has become the touchstone of priestly spirituality. But should such a practice be taken uncritically? For most Catholics who participate, is not the daily mass actually a privileged personal expression of devotion with holy communion as its seal? In their active, apostolic lives is not daily mass a thirty minute oasis of prayer? For this group, the Eucharist as an ecclesial and eschatological reality is hardly a felt concern.[11]

Writing about the same problem from another perspective, von Allmen discusses the Protestant abandonment of a weekly Sunday Eucharist:

> . . . the best way of exorcising the Reformed sabbatization of Sunday would be to restore to the Sunday service its true dimension by the celebration of the Eucharist. Sunday would not then be necessarily the day of rest (this would depend not on church decisions but on "worldly" decisions); instead,

11. García, "Contributions and Challenges" 371–72.

it would be the day of Communion. In this case we should also have to oppose the "Catholic" disqualification of Sunday, arising from monastic influence, and which consists in divorcing the Lord's Day from parochial Communion, not by failing to celebrate the Mass on Sundays, but by celebrating it on other days of the week or even on every day of the week. This too falsifies the nature of Sunday. The Protestant falsification of Sunday makes the latter parallel with the days of this world, thus neutralizing the eschatological tension in which the Church lives, and allowing the present aeon to absorb it; while the "Catholic" falsification of Sunday consists in making parallel with it those days [of the week] . . . ; this again neutralizes the eschatological tension of the Church, suggesting that it is already living in the future aeon.

Now it is important that—as the early Church so well understood—this eschatological tension should be respected, by a clear distinction between the Eucharistic day and the non-Eucharistic days. This does not mean that the present world is dismissed from view on Sundays. . . . But what qualifies Sunday as Sunday, what gives it color, is not rest from work, nor even the assembling of the people of God, but the assembling of the people of God for Eucharistic Communion. This is what makes Sunday Sunday, and if it is forgotten the nature of Sunday is lost.[12]

I apologize for quoting at such length, but I want to make sure that we realize that this is not just my idea or prejudice but a commonly recognized problem that merits serious reflection, consideration, and prayer. In fact, it is referred to obliquely and subtly in many works on the Eucharist, but so obliquely and subtly that the reference frequently escapes attention. A reality that is as much a part of the life of the Church as this practice surely is needs to be faced and discussed openly, or the consensus that we seek will never be reached.

These are the major questions that "Sunday Assembly in the Tradition" raises, at least in my mind and in the minds

12. von Allmen, *Worship: Its Theology and Practice* 226-27.

of authors I have read and other Christians I know. They present an awesome agenda. I hope they also make us more grateful than we sometimes feel for the great grace and gift we have in Sunday worship.

Sunday in the Eastern Tradition

ROBERT TAFT, S.J.

The title of this paper, "Sunday in the Eastern Tradition," is not entirely accurate. There are seven Eastern Christian liturgical traditions, not just one. However, they all share a common ethos, at least when contrasted with the West. So I shall speak about the most representative of these traditions, the Byzantine, to which the vast majority of Eastern Christians adhere. Most of them belong to the Eastern Orthodox Churches, but there are also some eight million Byzantine Catholics, if we count those in Rumania and the Soviet Ukraine who were forcibly incorporated into the Orthodox Church in the late 1940s.

The epithets "Eastern" or "Oriental" may conjure up visions of Bangkok and the Taj Mahal. But the Christian East is the Orient in the pre-Renaissance sense. It includes Southern Italy and Sicily, much of Yugoslavia, Bulgaria, Rumania, Greece, Asia Minor, as well as what we call the Middle East —in other words, the eastern half of the Mediterranean basin, cradle of our common Greco-Roman heritage. So we are talking about the Christianity of the Eastern patristic

ROBERT TAFT entered the Jesuits in 1949 and subsequently taught in Baghdad, Iraq. He later obtained a doctorate in Eastern Christian studies at the Pontifical Oriental Institute in Rome, where he is now ordinary professor of Oriental liturgy and languages. He is a visiting professor in the liturgical studies program at the University of Notre Dame.

world that is no more exotic or foreign than the Bible, which, after all, was written in Hebrew and Greek.

Like most great cultural traditions, the Byzantine Rite is a mongrel. At its basis lies the liturgical synthesis formed in the cathedral liturgy of Constantinople by the beginning of the eighth century. And in the monasteries of the capital, a new monastic synthesis was in formation under the leadership of the great Byzantine monastic reformer, St. Theodore Studites (d. 826). For the origins of the liturgy that came out of this monastic reform, we must look to Jerusalem. After the Persians destroyed the Holy City in 614, the monks of St. Sabas monastery in the wilderness near Jericho picked up the pieces and restored monastic life. As often happens after violent destruction, a remarkably creative period followed the holocaust, and a new monastic office was produced via a massive infusion of ecclesiastical poetry into the former staid and sober monastic psalmody. It is from this poetry that our present Byzantine liturgical anthology of Sunday propers, called the *Oktoichos*, or *Book of Eight Tones*, was formed.

To make a long story short, this Palestinian monastic synthesis was adopted by the Studite monasteries of Constantinople, and after the fall of the city to the Latins in 1204, this monastic office replaced the more elaborate cathedral rite even in the secular churches. So, for the celebration of Sunday in the Byzantine tradition, we have today a synthesis found in two sets of liturgical books: a native Constantinopolitan sacramentary (*Euchology*) and lectionaries; and a Book of Hours (*Horologion*) and its Sunday propers (*Oktoichos*), both of Jerusalem provenance.

To anyone beginning the study of Sunday in early Christian literature, the initial impression is one of confusion: Sunday is the first day, the day of creation, the day of light, the day of the new time. But it is also the last day, the eighth day, the day beyond days, the day of jubilee, the day of the end-time. It is the day of resurrection, but also the day of the post-resurrection appearances and meals. It is the day of the descent of the Spirit, day of the ascension, day of the assembly, day of the Eucharist, day of baptism, day of ordinations—until one asks, "Is there *anything* Sunday *doesn't* mean?" The answer, of course, is no. For in the Early Church, Sunday was indeed everything. It was *the* symbolic day, sign of the time of the Church between ascension and parousia, the time in which we are living now. It is the day symbolic of all days, for the purpose of all Christian liturgy is to express in a ritual moment that which should be the basic stance of every moment of our lives. Boone Porter has expressed this well in his little book on Sunday:

> All things in the Christian life are carried out in faith, hope, and charity, looking forward to the glory that is yet to be revealed. This is pre-eminently true of the Sunday gathering of the faithful. On the Eighth Day, the perpetual First Day of a new age, this view of eternity comes into focus. Then, in a particular sense, our heavenly citizenship is clearly and unequivocally affirmed. . . . Here we renew our allegiance each week to the Jerusalem that is above, here we are given some vision of the hope of our calling. On Sunday this is given to us not merely in homiletic exhortations to belief or catechetical declarations of the faith, but in the actual living experience of a full and comprehensive worship.[1]

It is this "living experience of a full and comprehensive worship" that characterizes Sunday in the Christian East. It is full because it still includes the complete cycle of cathedral services first synthesized in the Golden Age of the Fathers of the Church. It is comprehensive because it has retained the symbolic polyvalence of the pristine Lord's Day. Westerners are accustomed to thematic liturgies. Even ordinary Sundays in the Roman tradition were, until recently, feasts of the Trinity, with their proper preface. All this is foreign to the East, where such thematization, far from seeming an

1. H. B. Porter, *The Day of Light* (Greenwich, Conn., 1960) 81.

enrichment, would appear to limit the inexhaustible symbolic richness of the Sunday celebration to some topic of our choosing.

By and large, Eastern piety has remained free of the historical developments that in other places have led at times to the highlighting of relatively peripheral aspects of Christian devotional life. Consequently, the East's devotional storehouse has remained more or less uncluttered; its piety is still focused almost exclusively on the fundamentals of the faith. This is especially true of Sunday, which in the East has refused to be exploited for special interests not its own. It serves no purpose beyond itself. As such, it has the gratuitousness and uselessness of all symbol. It doesn't mean *something*; it simply *means*. It has no more use than art, or poetry, or a kiss. This is in radical contrast to contemporary narcissism regarding the worship of God: "I don't go to church because I don't get anything out of it." What one "*gets* out of it" is the inestimable privilege of glorifying God.

But if Sunday means everything, two of its themes stand out in the Byzantine tradition: day of light, day of the paschal mystery. The two poles of the liturgical expression of this reality in Christian antiquity were the vigil and the assembly for Word and Eucharist. Both have been preserved in the Byzantine tradition. I do not intend to concentrate on the Eucharist, because its meaning for Sunday is similar in all traditions. So, for the explication of these Sunday themes, let us turn to the vigil.

The "All-night Vigil" of the Byzantine tradition is originally a cathedral service comprising solemn vespers, the Sunday resurrection vigil, matins, and lauds, which in monasteries was drawn out through the night with long monastic psalmody. In parish worship this vigil is either split up, with vespers on Saturday evening and the rest before Sunday morning Mass, or—as in the Russian usage—it is celebrated as a unit Saturday evening, but without the long monastic

psalmody. In this abbreviated, parochial form it lasts at least
an hour and a half, and is a service of unparalleled beauty.

It opens in a flood of light and incense, as the doors of the
brilliantly illumined sanctuary are opened before the dark-
ened church, and the celebrant proclaims in solemn chant:
"Glory to the holy, consubstantial, and undivided Trinity,
now and always, and unto ages of ages!" No Byzantine service
begins without a blessing or glorification of the Holy Trinity,
the ultimate aim of all worship. Then the deacon and priest
call the congregation to prayer with verses adapted from
Psalm 94:6:

> Come let us adore our God and King!
> Come let us adore Christ our God and King!
> Come let us adore and fall down before the same Lord
>   Jesus Christ our God and King!
> Yes, come let us worship and bow down to him!

After this the deacon, lighting the way with a huge candle,
symbol of Christ who lights up our path, leads the celebrant
through the whole church incensing—really incensing, with
clouds of smoke, not just a few perfunctory swings of the
thurible from the distant sanctuary.

Meanwhile, the choir is chanting the invitatory psalm of
vespers, Psalm 103 (104), a psalm of creation. In the East,
liturgy is not just a service. It is also the place of theophany.
In the Sunday vigil, as in the Bible, the very first theophany
is creation. In chanting the invitatory psalm, special emphasis
is given to the christological theme of darkness and light,
which forms the base-symbolism of the cathedral office. The
psalm verses expressing this theme are repeated twice:

> The sun knows when to set; you bring darkness and it is night.
> How manifold are your works, O Lord! In wisdom, you wrought
>   them all!

This light theme is resumed immediately in the central rite of
evensong, the *lucernarium*, which opens with Psalm 140, the
heart of all Christian vesperal psalmody:

O Lord I cry to you: hear me O Lord!
Let my prayer rise like incense before you, my hands like the
    evening sacrifice.

While clouds of incense once again fill the church, sign of our
prayers rising to the throne of God, as the psalm says, every
candle in the church is lit, and the choir chants the proper
refrains with which the psalmody is farced, refrains showing
how the mystery of light that transforms creation is fulfilled
in the dying and rising of Christ. Here are some of the variable
refrains from the Sunday service in the third tone:[2]

> Everything has been enlightened by your resurrection, O
> Lord, and paradise has been opened again; all creation, ex-
> tolling you, offers to you the perpetual hymn of praise.

> We, who unworthily stay in your pure house, intone the even-
> ing hymn, crying from the depths: "O Christ our God, who has
> enlightened the world with your resurrection, free your peo-
> ple from your enemies, you who love humankind."

> O Christ, who through your Passion have darkened the sun,
> and with the light of your resurrection have illumined the
> universe: accept our evening hymn of praise, O you who love
> humankind.

> Your life-giving resurrection, O Lord, has illumined the whole
> world, and your own creation, which had been corrupted, has
> been called back. Therefore, freed from the curse of Adam, we
> cry: "O Lord almighty, glory to you."

> You underwent death, O Christ, so that you might free our
> race from death; and having risen from the dead on the third
> day, you raised with you those that acknowledge you as God,
> and you have illumined the world. O Lord, glory to you.

During the chanting of the final refrain, the priest and
deacon, bearing the smoking censor, walk in procession
through the church. On coming to the doors of the sanctuary,
they intone the age-old Hymn of Light, the *Phos hilaron*, which

2. English version adapted from *The Office of Vespers in the Byzantine Rite*
(London 1965) 42–43.

for over sixteen centuries, day after day, without variation or change, has proclaimed that the light of the world is not the sun of creation by day, nor the evening lamp by night, but the eternal Son of God, "the true light that enlightens everyone," in the words of the prologue of St. John's Gospel (1:9). I must confess that I find consolation in the company I am in when I intone this immortal hymn. St. Basil the Great, who quotes it in the fourth century, says it was already so old that no one remembers who composed it,[3] and Egeria surely heard it in Jerusalem around the same time. A literal version of the original Greek text reads:

> O joyous light of the holy glory of the immortal Father, heavenly, holy, blessed Jesus Christ!
> Having come to the setting of the sun, and beholding the evening light,
> We praise God Father, Son and Holy Spirit!
> It is fitting at all times that you be praised with auspicious voices, O Son of God, giver of life;
> That is why the whole world glorifies you![4]

The collect at the end of the vesperal intercessions resumes the themes of the service:

> O great and exalted God! You alone are immortal and dwell in unapproachable light! In your wisdom, you created the entire universe: You separated light from darkness, giving the sun charge of the day, and the moon and stars, the night. At this very hour, you permit us, sinful as we are, to approach you with our evening hymns of praise and glory. In your love for us, direct our prayers as incense in your sight, and accept them as a delightful fragrance. Throughout this present evening and the night that is to come, fill us with your peace. Clothe us in the armor of light. Rescue us from the terror of night. . . . Give us that sleep which you designed to soothe our weakness. . . . As we lie in bed this night, fill us with compunc-

3. *On the Holy Spirit* 29, 73, PG 32, 205.
4. Adapted from A. Tripolitis, "*Phos hilaron.* Ancient Hymn and Modern Enigma," *Vigiliae christianae* 24 (1970) 189.

tion, and enable us to keep your name in mind. Then, glad-
dened by your joy and enlightened by your precepts, may we
rise to glorify your goodness, imploring your great tenderness
of heart, not only for our own sins, but for those of all your
people. And for the sake of the Theotokos, touch all our lives
with your mercy. For you are good and full of love for us, O
God, and we give you glory, Father, Son, and Holy Spirit: now
and forever, and unto ages of ages, amen.[5]

In spite of its great solemnity, this is liturgy at its most
basic, taking the ordinary but universal fears and needs of
human life and turning them into theophany, signs of God.
The fear of darkness is a basic fear; the light that dispels it
is a need felt by all. "God is light," says the First Letter of
John (1:15), and this light shines in our world through the
transfigured face of Jesus Christ. This is a constant New
Testament theme, especially in the Johannine literature, but
also in the Pauline:

> John 1:4-5: In him was life, and the life was the light of men.
> The light shines in the darkness, and the darkness has not
> overcome it.
>
> John 8:12 (9:5): I am the light of the world; he who follows
> me will not walk in darkness, but will have the light of life.
>
> John 12:45-46: He who sees me sees him who sent me. I have
> come as light into the world, that whoever believes in me may
> not remain in darkness (cf. 12:35-36).
>
> Col 1:12-13: . . . (give) thanks to the Father, who has qualified
> us to share in the inheritance of the saints of light. He has
> delivered us from the dominion of darkness and transferred
> us to the kingdom of his beloved Son, in whom we have re-
> demption, the forgiveness of sins (cf. 1 Thess 5:5; Heb 6:4,
> 10:32).

Perhaps the most beautiful passage is the description
in Revelation 21:22-26 of the light of the Lamb in the heavenly city of God, the New Jerusalem:

---

5. *A Prayerbook* (Cambridge, N. Y.: New Skete, 1976) 198–199.

And I saw no temple in the city, for its temple is the Lord God
the Almighty and the Lamb. And the city has no need of sun
or moon to shine upon it, for the glory of God is its light, and
its lamp is the Lamb. By its light shall the nations walk; and
the kings of the earth shall bring their glory into it, and its
gates shall never be shut by day—and there shall be no night
there. . . .

The passage is a deliberate fulfillment of the prophecy of
Isaiah (60:1-3, 11, 19-20) in the prophet's vision of the restored Holy City of the Messianic times:

Arise, shine; for your light has come,
    And the glory of the Lord has risen upon you.
For behold, darkness shall cover the earth . . .
    but the Lord will arise upon you, and his glory
    will be seen upon you.
And the nations shall come to your light, and kings to
    the brightness of your rising. . . .
Your gates shall be open continually;
    day and night they shall not be shut. . . .
The sun shall be no more your light by day,
    nor for brightness shall the moon give light to
    you by night;
But the Lord will be your everlasting light,
    and your God will be your glory.
Your sun shall no more go down, nor your moon
    withdraw itself;
for the Lord will be your everlasting light,
    and your days of mourning shall be ended.

It was not long before this symbolism passed into the
poetry and hymnody of Christian worship. A venerable hymn
is cited in part in Ephesians 5:14. Clement of Alexandria (d.
215) in his *Exhortation to the Greeks* gives the full text:

Awake, O sleeper, and arise from the dead,
and Christ shall give you light,
    the sun of the resurrection,
    begotten before the morning star (Ps 109)
    who gives life by his own very rays.[6]

6. *Protrepticus 9, PG* 8, 196.

In Byzantine Sunday worship, this theme serves as symbolic matrix to express the unity of the Sunday mystery—the Passover of Christ—and its sacramental symbols: baptism, which in the Early Church was called *photismos* or "illumination," and Eucharist.

It is a theme that pervades all of Byzantine spirituality and mysticism. The life of the Spirit is an illumination by this divine light; to see God by this light is to live in him. St. Irenaeus wrote:

> To see the light is to be in the light and participate in its clarity; likewise to see God is to be in him and participate in his life-giving splendor; thus those who see God participate in his life.[7]

And in a moving passage of his Sermon on the Transfiguration, Anastasius of Sinai (d. *ca.* 700) has our transfigured Lord say:

> It is thus that the just shall shine at the resurrection. It is thus that they shall be glorified; into my condition they shall be transfigured, to this form, to this image, to this imprint, to this light and to this beatitude they shall be configured, and they shall reign with me, the Son of God.[8]

It is this symbolism that marks the rhythm of the hours in the Byzantine Office, evoking in the faithful a nostalgia for the divine vision which they are allowed to glimpse symbolically here on earth. It is a symbolism fulfilled in the Eucharist, as we hear in the refrain chanted after Communion:

> We have seen the true light! We have received the heavenly Spirit! . . .

---

7. *Adv. haer.* IV, 20, 5, *PG* 7, 1035.

8. A. Guillou, "Le Monastére de la Théotokes au Sinai. Origines; épiclese; mosaique de la Transfiguration; Homélie inédite d'Anastase le Sinaite sur la Transfiguration (étude et texte critique)," *Mélanges d'archéologie et d'histoire* 67 (1955) 253.

There is nothing specifically Eastern or Byzantine about all
of this—except that in the East it is still a living reality.

In the Sunday vigil, vespers is followed by matins, the
resurrection vigil, and lauds. The invitatory of matins, Psalm
117 in the Septuagint Greek, resumes once again the theme
of light and applies it to Christ:

> The Lord God is our light! Blessed is he who comes in the
> name of the Lord!
>
> *Verse*: Give thanks to the Lord, for he is good! Everlasting is
> his love!
>
> *Verse*: They surrounded me, they encircled me, but in the Lord's
> name I overcome them!
>
> *Verse*: No, I will not die; I will live, and declare the works of
> the Lord!
>
> *Verse*: The stone rejected by the builders has become the cor-
> nerstone; this is the Lord's doing, a marvel in our eyes![9]

In parish worship, the monastic psalmody of matins is
generally omitted, and one passes immediately to the three
psalms of the third nocturn, which on Saturday night is
transformed into the psalmody of the resurrection vigil described by Egeria (24:9-11), the *Apostolic Constitutions* (II, 59:
2-4), and other ancient sources. The elements of this service
are:

1) Three psalms in remembrance of the three days in the
   tomb;
2) An incensation in remembrance of the aromatic spices
   brought by the women to anoint the body of the Lord,
   thus inaugurating the first watch before the tomb,
   model of all Christian resurrection vigils, including
   what we call a wake.
3) A solemn proclamation of the Gospel of the resurrection, in remembrance of the angel who stood at the
   rolled-back stone of the tomb announcing the resurrection.

9. *Prayerbook*, 69.

Egeria describes this service as she saw it some 1600 years ago in the rotunda of the resurrection in Jerusalem:

> But on the seventh day, the Lord's Day, there gather in the courtyard before cock-crow all the people, as many as can get in, as if it were Easter. . . . Soon the first cock crows, and at that the bishop enters, and goes into the cave in the Anastasis. The doors are all opened, and all the people come into the Anastasis, which is already ablaze with lamps. When they are inside, a psalm is said by one of the presbyters, with everyone responding, and it is followed by a prayer; then a psalm is said by one of the deacons, and another prayer; then a third psalm is said by one of the clergy, a third prayer, and the Commemoration of All. After these three psalms and prayers they take censers into the cave of the Anastasis, so that the whole Anastasis basilica is filled with the smell. Then the bishop, standing inside the screen, takes the Gospel book and goes to the door, where he himself reads the account of the Lord's resurrection. At the beginning of the reading the whole assembly groans and laments at all that the Lord underwent for us, and the way they weep would move even the hardest heart to tears. When the Gospel is finished, the bishop comes out, and is taken with singing to the Cross, and they all go with him. They have one psalm there and a prayer, then he blesses the people, and that is the dismissal.[10]

In the Byzantine tradition the present vigil opens with the solemn chanting of select verses from Psalms 134, 135, and 118, accompanied by refrains of the myrrh-bearing women, those who went to the tomb to anoint the body of the Lord and thus became the first witnesses of the resurrection. As soon as the choir intones "Praise the name of the Lord" from Psalm 134, the doors of the sanctuary are opened, all the lights and candles in the church are lit, and the celebrant, preceded once more by the deacon and his candle, incenses again the whole church. The refrains of the myrrhbearers give the sense of this service:

10. J. Wilkinson, *Egeria's Travels* (London 1971) 124–125.

By the tomb stood an angel radiant in light, and thus did he speak to the myrrh-bearing women: "Let not your sorrow mingle tears with precious ointment. You see the tomb before you; look for yourselves. He is not here; he has risen!"

With the first rays of dawn they had set out for the tomb, sobbing and lamenting as they walked along. But when they reached the tomb, they were startled by an angel who said: "The time for tears and sorrow is now over. Go! Tell his friends that he has risen!"

Your women friends had come with ointment, Lord, hoping to anoint your bruised and battered body cold in death. But the angel stood before them, saying: "Why seek the living among the dead? He is God! He has risen from the grave."

There follow the responsory and the solemn chanting of the Gospel of the resurrection, after which the gospel book is solemnly borne in procession to the center of the church and enthroned there, while the choir sings the resurrection hymn professing faith that, having heard the paschal Gospel, we too have seen and tasted the glory of God:

Having seen Christ's resurrection, let us adore the holy Lord Jesus Christ, who is alone without sin. We worship your cross, O Christ, we sing and tell the glory of your holy resurrection. For you are our God, we know of no other than you, we call on your name. Come all you faithful, let us worship Christ's holy resurrection. For behold, through the cross has joy come to all the world. As we continually bless the Lord, we sing of his resurrection, for he has endured the cross and destroyed death by death.[11]

After the intercessions, one of the eight Canons of the Resurrection is chanted according to the Sunday tone, while the faithful come up to venerate the Gospel, be anointed with aromatic oil, and receive a piece of blessed bread, signs of the fortitude needed in the true vigil, the vigil of life.

11. *Prayerbook*, 110–111.

The same themes of light and paschal triumph are found throughout the rich poetry of lauds, especially in the odes of the canon, a series of refrains composed according to the themes of the biblical canticles. I do not have time to describe all this, but the same realities are proclaimed: darkness and light; the darkness of sin overcome by the illumination of the risen Christ.

Equally important liturgically is that these realities are not just affirmed *pro forma*, in a ho-hum sort of way. They are shouted and chanted and hymned. They are woven into a scenario of poetry and procession, movement and rest, darkness and light, smoke and symbol and song, so that the casual visitor is often a bit overwhelmed, and would be moved to say, "Why, they really believe all that!" And, indeed, they do. The Vatican II Constitution on the Sacred Liturgy (no. 2) calls the liturgy "the outstanding means by which the faithful can express in their lives and manifest to others the mystery of Christ and the real nature of the true Church." A concrete example of what this means can be seen on any Sunday in the Eastern tradition. One of my favorite anecdotes comes from the Eastern marches of Poland between the two world wars. A Polish Catholic picked up in his carriage a poor Orthodox peasant-priest who was trudging along the dirt road on foot, and engaged him in spiritual discourse, somewhat in the polemic tones of those pre-ecumenical times. What was important, the Latin said, was the conversion of sinners, confession, catechism, prayer. The Orthodox were too involved with ritual, which is secondary to the real ministry of the Church. The Orthodox priest replied with great dignity:

> Among you it is indeed only an accessory. Among us Orthodox (and at these words he blessed himself) it is not so. The liturgy is our common prayer, it initiates our faithful into the mystery of Christ better than all your catechism. It passes before our eyes the life of our Christ, the Russian Christ, and that can

be understood only in common, at our holy rites, in the mystery of our icons. When one sins, one sins alone. But to understand the mystery of the Risen Christ, neither your books nor your sermons are of any help. For that, one must have lived with the Orthodox Church the Joyous Night (of Easter). And he blessed himself again.[12]

The story refers to the Easter vigil, but this same liturgical spirit characterizes every Sunday vigil, and indeed all worship, in the Byzantine East. Throughout all the vicissitudes of its history, the Christian East has preserved a continuity of faith and worship, rooted in the resurrection and hope of the world to come, that has sustained its faithful during the dark ages of oppression. Political circumstances have often deprived the Eastern Churches of the need or possibility of developing the more active apostolic activities that are so integral to Church life and organization in the West. But as long as the mysteries can be celebrated, the Church lives, held together not by organization nor authority nor education, but by communion year after year in the regular cycle of feast and fast.

Peter Hammond, in his moving account of the Greek Church after World War II, has expressed in striking terms the hold that worship has on the Christian of the East:

Nobody who has lived and worshipped amongst Greek Christians for any length of time but has sensed in some measure the extraordinary hold which the recurring cycle of the Church's liturgy has upon the piety of the common people. Nobody who has kept great lent with the Greek Church, who has shared in the fast which lies heavy upon the whole nation for forty days; who has stood for long hours, one of an innumerable multitude who crowd the tiny Byzantine churches of Athens and overflow into the streets, while the familiar pattern of God's saving economy towards man is re-presented in psalm and prophecy, in lections from the Gospel, and the

12. C. Bourgeois, S.J., "Chez les paysans de la Podlachie et du nord-est de la Pologne. Mai 1924—décembre 1925," *Etudes* 191 (1927) 585.

matchless poetry of the canons; who has known the desolation of the holy and great Friday, when every bell in Greece tolls its lament and the body of the Saviour lies shrouded in flowers in all the village churches throughout the land; who has been present at the kindling of the new fire and tasted of the joy of a world released from the bondage of sin and death—none can have lived through all this and not have realized that for the Greek Christian the Gospel is inseparably linked with the liturgy that is unfolded week by week in his parish church. Not among the Greeks only but throughout Orthodox Christendom the liturgy has remained at the very heart of the Church's life.[13]

And all of this permeates the everyday lives of the people in a way that liturgy has long ceased to do in most other traditions. Eastern Christians have a sense of ownership and pride in their rite. It is their church, their tradition, their community, bound up with their whole history and culture. There is no separation between piety and liturgy. If you asked Eastern Christians which of their devotions were "liturgical," they would not know what you were talking about. It's all one thing, liturgy and personal piety, and it still marks the rhythm of daily life. I like to have my Eastern students write an essay on what their tradition means to them. Here is a typical passage from such an essay, written by a young American layman of the Ukrainian Catholic Church:

> To be in the center of the crowd that pushes forward to kiss the cross on some major feast day, each waiting to have the head anointed and maybe to exchange a few words with the priest—you know you are surrounded by people that would never be satisfied with the almost furtive handshakes that are exchanged in Latin churches during the Rite of Peace. But the enthusiasm of the tradition doesn't end in the church building. In many ways it is carried into the daily lives of the people. The icons one finds in homes are one way this is done: the same saints one sees in church one also sees in the kitchen

13. P. Hammond, *The Waters of Marah. The Present State of the Greek Church* (London 1956) 51-52.

or bedroom, often with a burning candle and a decorative scarf. On great feasts there are the blessings of things we use every day—water on Theophany, fruit on Transfiguration, herbs and flowers on Dormition. These things are taken home and used: the water is drunk, the fruit is eaten, and the flowers decorate the table for several days.

So much for liturgy. I began there deliberately, because in the East that is where one always begins. There, liturgy is not one of the many things the Church does. It is its very life. One might ask, of course, what relevance all this has today. I can only refer to my own experience, and to the testimony of others who can in no way be accused of living in a romantic cloud of incense divorced from the realities of the modern world. One is Olivier Clément, contemporary French writer and lay theologian converted at the age of 27 from atheism. He chose Orthodoxy because, in his own words, "I was hungry for a Church that was above all Eucharist. For a community which professed to be the Body of Christ in the Eucharist. For a theology that flowed from the chalice. It was then that I met the Orthodox."[14] More telling, perhaps, is the witness of Tatiana Goricheva, feminist and activist of the Christian renewal movement in Leningrad, expelled from the Soviet Union in July 1980. Born in 1947 of atheist parents, she knew absolutely nothing about religion, had never even been inside a church. Then she visited an Orthodox church and discovered the liturgy:

> I was enchanted by the liturgy, by the beauty of the rite. . . .
> I did not want to leave church after the liturgical celebrations.
> It seemed like leaving paradise to fall back into hell. I was
> overwhelmed and won over by all that not because of any
> estheticism, but on the level of religious ontology, so to speak,
> and not on the level of sentimentality.[15]

14. O. Clément, *L'autre soleil. Quelques notes d'autobiographie spirituelle* (Paris 1975) 142.

15. P. Modesto, "Intervista a Tat'jana Goriceva," *Russia cristiana* 2 (176) anno 6 (March–April 1981) 58.

My message is not that Western Christians should all rush out and head East. The Christian East has its bad side too. But it is presumably the good qualities that Westerners wish to learn from. What are some of the good things we have seen in the Eastern tradition of Sunday that the Western Christian could reflect on with profit?

1) Sunday is not just Eucharist. If all you have on Sunday is Eucharist, then you're offering a feast with only the main course. I think what I have said about the vigil illustrates that clearly enough.

2) Liturgy is *liturgy*, the common service of the People of God. Let me illustrate what I mean with a couple of personal experiences. One Sunday in July 1966 I found myself in Timosoara, capital of the Banat in Western Rumania, and decided to attend the Sunday liturgy in the Orthodox cathedral. I call it *the* Sunday liturgy because there was only one. It was concelebrated by three presbyters and two deacons. Since it was not a feast day, the archbishop was not celebrating, but presided from his throne in the nave. The rest of the clergy assisted from the choir. Needless to say, this was *their* Sunday Eucharist, too, and not some sort of conventual or chapter Mass at which they were obliged to be present *pro forma*, following the private celebration of *their* Mass! This was it: their Mass, the bishop's Mass, the cathedral Mass, everybody's Mass. One people, one community, one church, one liturgy.

This year on Palm Sunday I was in a Catholic retreat house. I asked about Sunday Mass, received a perplexed stare that said, "But aren't you a priest?" and was informed that there was a Mass "for the people" at 7:30 AM. Since I entertain the illusion that I'm people, I allowed myself to attend. The celebration commenced with the celebrant announcing that there would be no sermon because of the length of the Gospel (as it turned out, the whole service lasted exactly thirty-eight minutes). I won't go into all the details. The celebrant did everything alone, including all the readings. Hosts were consecrated at the Mass, but that was not for us. We were given Communion from the tabernacle, after which the freshly consecrated hosts were reserved for the following week. Although the retreat house was full, very few were at this Mass. During it, however, several priests were saying private (i.e., solitary) Masses on both sides of the same chapel. And all day long, other groups were doing their thing. Palms were blessed at two other Masses. But it was all so divisive, so fragmented. The simple, "non-groupie" Christian who just wanted Palm Sunday community worship could not find it because it was not to be had. Everyone worshiped God, everyone was doing something, but they did not come together to do it; they split.

The point I'm making is that nowhere in the Eastern Church could that scene have taken place. And I know of no cathedral of the Roman Catholic Church where the Timoşoara cathedral scene could have taken place. And that's part of what is wrong with Western Catholic liturgy. It's too often a private party.

3) Eastern Sunday worship is *traditional*. It is always the same familiar liturgy. Week after week the same invitatories open the services, the incensations are always done in the same place and in the same way, the Litany of Peace prays for the same basic needs. Psalm 140 and the Hymn of Light are always the heart of vespers. After the vigil Gospel, the same resurrection hymn is sung. Of course there are numerous variable parts, but that's the problem of the clergy and choir. Everything is *familiar*, it's *ours*, we *know* it. It's not boring because it is magnificent, and it is done well. So, from my experience, I am tempted to think that the contemporary Western mania for variety in liturgy is because the liturgy is often done so poorly—sometimes appallingly so—that people are scrambling to escape the impasse by forever trying something new. Someone once asked me how to plan an Easter

liturgy. I suggested some old standbys, like the paschal candle. "We did that last year" was the answer I got. Well, Christians have been doing a lot of things for almost two thousand years, and I hope we keep it up until the parousia. The answer is not to replace what we do, but to do it as if we meant it. Nor do we need to go East for examples of what I'm trying to propose. Right here at Notre Dame we have the same familiar evensong every Sunday, year in and year out, and nobody complains, because it is *good!* Indeed, one of the reasons it is good is because it is familiar, and hence viable. Variety is not the answer to trash.

4) Eastern Sunday liturgy is traditional also because it is *focused.* There is really only one basic theme: Jesus Christ died and rose for our salvation, and is with us all days even unto the end of time. But I said enough about this point above.

5) Many other characteristics could be highlighted. One final one must be mentioned, however: Eastern worship has a sense of *transcendence.* This is true not only of the liturgy itself but of the whole atmosphere of sacredness and mystery that surrounds its every movement and communicates a sense of reverential awe. In the creation of this spirit, it would be hard to exaggerate the importance of the church and its iconography. To see a Byzantine liturgy in a properly appointed Byzantine church is to cross the threshold to another world, or rather to this world made visible in its redeemed reality as the transfigured cosmos beyond time.

This is why icons are called windows to another world, why the most humble village church is "heaven on earth," according to St. Germanus of Constantinople, "the place where the God of Heaven dwells and moves"; where one can "lay aside all worldly care," as the Cherubic Hymn enjoins, "to receive the King of all." It is the heavenly sanctuary "where men and women, according to their capacity and desire, are caught up into the adoring worship of the redeemed cosmos; where dogmas are no barren abstractions but hymns of exulting praise."[16]

Christians chanting the liturgy in this atmosphere, as clouds of incense rise with their prayers toward Christ-Pantocrator depicted in the dome, are in the world of the Fathers of the Church. Their theology of visible creation as a symbol of the invisible, of the incarnation as the icon-restorer of the reflection of divine beauty to humankind, is what makes Christian iconography and liturgical symbolism possible. For in the East, iconography and liturgy have the same quality. The liturgy is not a "ceremony"; it is an object of contemplation, an awesome vision full of mystery, before which one prostrates in reverential awe.

Worshiping in this atmosphere of profuse symbolism through which the supernatural splendor of the inaccessible divine majesty is approached, Eastern Christians witness the exaltation and sanctification of creation, the majestic appearance of God who enters us, sanctifies us, divinizes us through the transfiguring light of his heavenly grace. It is not only a matter of receiving the sacraments, but also one of living habitually within a liturgical atmosphere which stirs us in body and soul in order to transform us before a vision of spiritual beauty and joy.

Our lowliness and unworthiness, when faced with such an intense liturgical expression of the unsearchable majesty of God, might be forbidding were it not for the deep Christianity of the Byzantine liturgical prayers. The glory of the Lord and his incomparable transcendence, our lowliness and sinfulness—these themes lead us to a deep sense of reverence and humility. "Lord have mercy!" is the congregation's incessant refrain to the diaconal petitions. These sentiments find balance, however, in another constantly repeated theme:

16. Hammond, *Waters of Marah*, 16.

Christ is the Ruler of All, to be sure; but he is also the divine philanthropist, the "lover of humankind" who poured himself out for our salvation.

Not only in the prayers of the priest but also in the exclamations to which the people respond with their "Amen," this balance between glorification and tender love is a constantly alternating refrain.

> For You are a good God and You love humankind, and we give glory to You. . . .
> Again and again we bow down before You and we beseech You, O gracious lover of humankind. . . .
> To You, O Lord and lover of humankind, we commend our whole life and hope. . . .

So there is not just majesty and awe, but also an integrity and equilibrium, a sense of the balanced wholeness of things. The liturgy is transcendent but not distant, hieratic but not clericalized, communal but not impersonal, traditional but not formalistic.

Apart from this liturgical ethos I have been describing, several nonreligious factors on the sociological and historical level also contribute to making Sunday what it is in the Eastern traditions. For most Eastern Christians, the Church has become and remains the symbol of their national identity, especially in areas such as Serbia, Greece, Macedonia, and the Middle East, where centuries of Ottoman tyranny left the people with no other bastion of communal self-identity and self-respect apart from the Church.

A second factor is that of size. Most Eastern congregations are small, and by Western standards most Eastern church buildings are small. This has considerable impact on the dramatic and tangible aspects of liturgical prayer: its movement and staging, its choreography, and their effect. Many medieval Byzantine churches were no more than thirty feet long. Perhaps this miniaturization reflected the desire for a more intimate worship to counteract the shift from the classical openness of the early liturgy to the more remote and inaccessible cult of medieval Byzantine monasticism.[17] At any rate, this smallness helps dispel the anonymity of the modern parish community, and this is not just an old world phenomenon. On the contrary, it is even reinforced in the diaspora, where the parish often remains the last bastion of ethnic community life.

After the Sunday morning liturgy in many churches in the U.S., there is a rush to the parking lot as if someone had yelled "Fire!" This is not true in most Eastern parishes. Everyone mills around outside when the weather is good, and chats. In smaller parishes there is a coffee hour in the parish hall. This hall is an essential component of the parish plant, and the focus of all sorts of activities. Even the often unreachable young seem drawn by this togetherness. (On a recent lecture tour among the Ukrainian Catholic communities of Western Canada, I stayed at the rectory of the Ukrainian Redemptorists in Saskatoon. The place was overrun by teenagers coming for various meetings during the few days I was there.)

Another exemplary Eastern community is in nearby Chicago, at the Ukrainian Catholic Church of Saints Volodymyr and Olha. This parish in the old, inner-city Ukrainian neighborhood was chosen as the subject of a program on public television a few years ago. Not only is there a beautiful new church building completely decorated with frescoes in the traditional style, but this parish has become the nucleus of urban renewal for the whole area. People who had moved to the suburbs have been drawn back to the old neighborhood. Old buildings have been bought up, renovated, and turned into housing for the aged, for the clergy, for seminarians. In the basement of the church is the parish hall, where lectures and banquets and other social and cultural affairs are

---

17. See T. F. Mathews, "'Private' Liturgy in Byzantine Architecture: Toward a Re-appraisal," *Cahiers archéologiques* (at press).

held in dizzying succession. Behind the church there is a youth center with its own building. In still another parish building there is a Ukrainian cultural center where several young men studying for the priesthood are in residence and share intimately in the life of the community. Across the street from the church is the old folks' home, also run by the parish.

And there is the liturgy. The choir is superb, and esthetically the services are some of the purest and best Eastern liturgy in the Western hemisphere. The Sunday I was there, vespers on Saturday evening lasted for about an hour. Then there was a buffet supper in the parish hall, at which I gave a lecture to the audience of about two hundred, including many families and young people. On Sunday morning, matins of the resurrection began at eight, followed immediately by the Eucharist. These morning services, done in Ukrainian with great reverence and devotion, lasted about two hours.

Of course one will immediately protest: "*One* hour Saturday evening, *two* more on Sunday morning—who will put up with that?" Some not only put up with it, they demand it. Others come for only part of it, according to their devotion, but even they would be the last to say it should be cut down or omitted. Liturgy in the East is like liturgy in a monastery. It has an indivisible quality, an objectivity which demands that the cycle of prayer be accomplished in its integrity. This *opus Dei* is primarily the work of the community as a whole, and not of its individual members. The fact that some cannot or will not participate in all of it is not an argument for its suppression. So, in Eastern churches, people drift in and out of services according to their fervor and need. In Chicago, for example, many were there throughout vespers Saturday evening, while very few were present at the start of matins early Sunday morning. But gradually people drifted in, and the church was almost full by the time the Eucharist got under way.

Furthermore, when reacting with horror at the thought of so much liturgy, we should be careful—especially in this campus setting—with our judgments of what modern Americans will or will not put up with. Teenagers will wait in line outside all night in bad weather to buy tickets to a rock concert. And, by tradition, Notre Dame students stand—stand, not sit—throughout the entire two-and-a-half to three hours of every home football game. People will give time to whatever is important in their life: rock concerts, football, or the glorification of almighty God.

Of course I have been describing an ideal. In many parishes the tradition has cracked under the customary strains of urban secular life. So we must not deceive ourselves, as some Orthodox writers do when they contrast Eastern "Eucharistic" ecclesiology, rooted in the communion of the Body of Christ, with what they call the "legalistic" ecclesiology of the West. Archimandrite Kallistos (Timothy) Ware, Anglican convert to Orthodoxy, writes of "Western secularism," and affirms: "We are present in the Western world above all as a celebrating community, a Eucharistic communion, a people of prayer."[18] That is all very beautiful, but one wonders what a "Eucharistic" ecclesiology can mean in churches where practically no one goes to Communion more than a few times a year. Or why secularism is "Western" when—according to their own statistics—in the region of Athens, where one-third of all Greeks live, only 9 percent go to church every Sunday, and even these figures can be considered generous.[19] Other statistics put Greek-Orthodox Sunday practice at about 6 percent in the villages and 5 percent in

---

18. K. Ware, "The Meaning of the Great Fast," in *The Lenten Triodion*, trans. Mother Mary and K. Ware (London and Boston 1978) 15. The second citation is from *Episkepsis* (Bulletin of the Orthodox Center of the Ecumenical Patriarchate, Chambésy-Geneva) no. 246 (February 15, 1981) 7.

19. *Episkepsis*, no. 240 (November 1, 1980) 8.

urban areas, with twice as many women in church as men.[20] Among the Orthodox Balkan Slavs, the weekly attendance is even less.[21] By contrast, in the supposedly "secular" West, in France, where religious practice is notoriously low, 12 percent of the Catholics go to church regularly.[22] And in West Germany, 30 percent attend Sunday Mass.[23] So much for "Western" secularism and Orthodox witness in the West as a Eucharistic community of prayer! Among Eastern Catholics the percentage of those who regularly practice and communicate is much higher. But honesty forces us to admit that although the Eastern Churches have a glorious heritage still observable in their Sunday liturgical and social observances, they could learn a thing or two from the Catholic West about getting the people to church and to Communion.

So we all have something to learn from one another. That is why the ultimate answer to our problems is the one that Christ started out with in the first place: the union of all in him.

20. M. Rinvolucri, *The Anatomy of a Church: Greek Orthodoxy Today* (New York 1966) 27.

21. *Ibid.* 177, and my own observations in Serbia and Macedonia.

22. *Informations catholiques internationales* no. 548 (March 15, 1980) 13, 15.

23. *Ibid.* no. 557 (December 15, 1980) 34.

Catholic Sunday in America:
Its Shape and Early History

JOHN GURRIERI

Describing the Roman Catholic liturgical movement of the twentieth century in *A Religious History of the American People*, Sydney E. Ahlstrom maintains that the "liturgical apostolate" of the fifties was needed "not only for intensified study in the seminaries, but for a deepening of the laity's understanding through the publication of English translations of the missal, for the encouragement of congregational participation, for the reconceiving of liturgical ceremony and church architecture to make this possible, for the wider use of the vernacular and preaching in worship, and for the renewal of private devotional life."[1] While Ahlstrom and other commentators may be correct in the general assumption which lies behind this statement, recent studies in the history of

1. Sydney E. Ahlstrom, *A Religious History of the American People*, 2 vols. (Garden City, N.Y., 1975) 1:523.

JOHN GURRIERI is a priest of the diocese of Brooklyn. After some years of parish work, he went on to earn a doctorate in liturgical studies at the Institut Superieur de Liturgie in Paris. Since then he has taught at Immaculate Conception Seminary in Huntington, New York, and at The Catholic University in Washington, D.C. He is currently executive director of the Secretariat of the Bishops' Committee on the Liturgy.

liturgy in America are beginning to dispel the notion that interest in the liturgy and in liturgical spirituality has no prehistory in the United States before the liturgical movement formally began in this country.

For one, "English translations of the missal" have been in the hands of American Catholics since at least 1740 when Bishop Richard Challoner of London, under whose canonical jurisdiction England's American colonies were directed, published *The Garden of the Soul*, a manual of devotion containing the Ordinary of the Mass in Latin-English columns side by side. Likewise, concern for "congregational participation" at Mass was already found in late-eighteenth-century America, just as concern for the "wider use of the vernacular and preaching in worship" has its precedent in the apostolate of the itinerant Spanish Franciscan friars in Texas, New Mexico, and California, the French missionaries who accompanied fur trappers and explorers in the wilderness of New France, the Maryland Jesuits establishing churches in Lord Baltimore's "Catholick Colonie," and, of course, in Bishop John Carroll's early and repeatedly expressed desires for the entire liturgy in the English language.[2]

Misconceptions about liturgy in the United States by historians and foreign observers are not new. Wrong estimates result primarily because hardly anyone in the field of American Church history or liturgical studies has bothered to look into American liturgical history, or even to consider that liturgy in America is a fruitful area of research. Such lack of concern and interest is beginning to change, but only just beginning. Historians of late have shown an interest in American Catholic devotional life, "Catholic revivalism,"

---

2. Cf. John Tracy Ellis, "Archbishop Carroll and the Liturgy in the Vernacular" in *Perspectives in American Catholicism*, Benedictine Studies 5 (Baltimore, 1963) 127–133. Cf. James Hennesey, *American Catholics: A History of the Roman Catholic Community in the United States* (New York, 1981) 84–85.

and related issues.[3] No one, however, has really studied the *liturgical* life of Catholics in America. What do we know, for example, about the American Catholic perception of the word *liturgy* in the eighteenth and nineteenth centuries? Where does one find information about the style of liturgical celebrations, or what Sunday looked like in a typical urban or rural parish in any part of this country in that period? In the classic studies of American Catholicism little, if anything, is to be found on the liturgical life of Americans. American Church history, like its European counterpart, has been a narrative study of relationships between Church and State, between Catholic and Protestant; a story of authority conflict, or the lives of "great figures" whose greatness often emanated from their ability to consolidate the "Catholic position" in the United States; and, if these figures are bishops, what they did for Catholics as pastors leading worship, or directing the liturgical and devotional life of their churches.

My purpose in this essay is neither to denigrate the great Catholic historians from John Gilmary Shea to Peter Guilday to John Tracy Ellis, nor to pose as a historian with credentials to change the direction of American Catholic historiography. Rather, I wish to single out one particular aspect of Catholic liturgical practice in the United States—Sunday worship—and indicate a few possible areas of research and reflection. My question is this: From the time Catholicism was introduced into America by Spanish, French, and English colonists, how did Catholics spend their time on Sunday? Correlative to this question are some others: What were the sources which influenced the shape of Sunday in America from the seventeenth century to the beginnings of the liturgical move-

3. Cf. Jay P. Dolan, *Catholic Revivalism: The American Experience, 1830–1900* (Notre Dame, Ind., 1978); Jay P. Dolan, "American Catholics and Revival Religion, 1850–1900," *Horizons*, Journal of the College of Theology Society, 3 (Spring 1976) 39–57; Joseph P. Chinnici, "Organization of the Spiritual Life: American Catholic Devotional Works, 1791–1866," *Theological Studies* 40 (June 1979) 229–255; John Cogley, *Catholic America* (Garden City, N.Y., 1974).

ment in Dom Virgil Michel's time (1890–1938)? Will reflection on the past shed light on the current crisis of Sunday
worship in a postconciliar period of liturgical fatigue?

I. JOHN CARROLL'S LITURGICAL VIEWS

In 1789, a month after George Washington was inaugurated
as the new Republic's first president, America's priests elected
John Carroll as first bishop of the Catholic Church in the
United States. Carroll's election was confirmed by Pius VI
on November 6 of that year. (At the same time the Pope
created the diocese of Baltimore, which included the thirteen
states and all American territories.) On August 15, 1790,
this descendant of an old Maryland family was consecrated
bishop. Carroll had, of course, been superior of the American
missions since 1784. As his correspondence and writings
show,[4] the five years before his episcopal ordination were
years of consolidating a nearly chaotic situation in an as-yet-
unorganized Church. In the fall of 1784, shortly after his
appointment, and while he was trying to organize a ram-
bunctious and independent presbyterate and laity in his far-
flung jurisdiction, he already found it necessary to defend
the Church against the attacks of Charles Wharton, a Maryland Jesuit who had left the ministry. Wharton's "problems"
ranged from papal infallibility to transubstantiation.[5]

   In *An Address to the Roman Catholics of the United States of America*,
Carroll attempted systematically to refute each of Wharton's
charges against Roman Catholic doctrine. What is more
interesting about the *Address* than Carroll's familiarity with
patristic, conciliar, and medieval sources is his application
of the principal *lex orandi, lex credendi* when defending the doctrine of the real presence. After marshalling John Chrysos-

---

   4. Thomas O'Brien Hanley, *The John Carroll Papers*, 3 vols. (Notre Dame,
Ind., 1976).
   5. *The John Carroll Papers* 1:82–144.

tom, Augustine, Gregory Nazianzen, and others to his side, he cites "an authority still more authentic, the public liturgy of the Church of Constantinople." He goes on to demonstrate from the structure of the Byzantine liturgy, its texts and even its rubrics, the veracity of the real presence. "Thus is proved the adoration of Christ in the Eucharist, not only from the testimony of the Fathers, but by a law of ecclesiastical discipline, connected with daily and inviolable practice; and making part of the worship rendered to Jesus Christ agreeable to the public liturgy; and consequently," he concludes, "the primitive belief of the real presence is fully established."[6]

Of interest in this text, as in so many other of Carroll's writings, is a genuine concern and love for the liturgy, and an ability to see in the Church's worship the Church's law of belief. The American Church was fortunate in having as its first bishop not only a man who could correspond and converse with the shapers of the new Republic, but a pastor who believed the Sunday Eucharistic liturgy to be the core of Christian life from which and to which Christian doctrine, spirituality, and the Church's relationship to the world ebbed and flowed, and to which Catholics brought their whole being.

In this same context, the future bishop of Baltimore expressed the need for a vernacular liturgy on Sunday in which the congregation could participate fully in word and song. "The great part of our congregations must be utterly ignorant of the meaning and sense of the public offices of the Church," he wrote to an English friend, the Reverend Joseph Berington in 1787. For, "to continue the practice of the Latin Liturgy

---

6. *Ibid.* 127. Carroll's "Address to Roman Catholics on Wharton" demonstrates a broad familiarity not only with the Fathers of the Church but also with the early medieval controversialists Peter Lombard, Thomas, and the post-Tridentine theologians on the whole subject of transubstantiation and other questions raised by Wharton.

in the present state of things must be owing to chimerical
fears of innovation or to indolence and inattention in the first
pastors of the national Churches in not joining to solicit or
indeed ordain this necessary alteration."[7]

While Carroll was later to give up views on the vernacular
question (there was no hope of change), "the present state of
things" in the new American Church led him firmly to believe
that in a people's liturgy, as opposed to a clerical order of
worship, American Catholics would find themselves close to
one another while being sensitive to the need for unity and
harmony with the non-Catholic majority.

II. Early Liturgical and Devotional Books

Knowing the thinking of the nation's first bishop on matters
liturgical is certainly not the same as learning what Sunday
worship was like in his time, unless one is simultaneously
familiar with the actual situation in parishes between 1789
and 1815, the years of Carroll's episcopate. Needless to say,
no empirical research has come down to us from that period.
Nor were there many observers or pundits around in those
days who facilely tossed off a column on the "state of the
liturgy" in a newspaper or some other periodical. Where
then does one obtain some hard data and information about
the practice of Sunday liturgy in early America?

There is a great deal of archeological and literary evidence
which sheds at least some light on our subject. Church buildings can tell us much about seating patterns for the assembly
and choir, the choreography of processions, the place and
movement of ministers. The attitudes of Catholics toward
the liturgy can be exemplified also by the materials used for
liturgical vestments, artifacts, and appointments. A mono-
graph or two would be most welcome on the relationship

---

7. Carroll to Berington, cited by Ellis (cf. n. 2 above) 129.

between liturgy and such archeological evidence. One can also turn to periodicals and correspondence for some information on the liturgy. Such a task would be enormous, since nothing has yet been done. However, there is also the evidence and testimony of the *liturgical* literature of American Catholicism, that is, the liturgical and devotional *books* which actually were in the hands of worshipers, thumbed through and used in church and at home. Also included in this category are various hymnals and collections of music compiled for use in the liturgy. My reflections are based on such material: what books did Catholics use when they "went to Mass" on Sunday? what books shaped their thinking, spirituality, and liturgical patterns? what do these books tell us about our ancestors in faith?

Centering in on Anglo-American Catholics, the first thing we discover is that liturgical and devotional books available to them were English in both authorship and publication. "Catholic printing" in America did not really begin until the third decade of the eighteenth century, most probably in Philadelphia.[8] To understand, therefore, the history of liturgy in colonial and republican America, one must turn to both English and American books of a devotional or liturgical nature. From these, a great deal can be learned about the "Catholic Sunday in America," its shape and history.

8. Cf. Wilfrid J. Parsons, *Early Catholic Americana: A List of Books and Other Works by Catholic Authors in the United States, 1729–1830* (New York, 1939); John A. Gurrieri, "Holy Days in America," *Worship* 54 (September 1980) 428, n. 31. However, as Parsons demonstrates, Catholic books were printed elsewhere in this same period: Germantown, Pennsylvania, where works in the German language were published for Catholics, e.g., Thomas à Kempis, *Das kleine A.B.C. in der Schule Christi. . .* (1742) (Parsons, p. 2); in Boston, where "A Hymn of St. Bernard's to the Holy Jesus" was published by B. Green in 1744 (Parsons, p. 2). In the latter part of the eighteenth century both Baltimore and New York would become increasingly important centers of Catholic printing, eventually superceding Philadelphia. Baltimore especially would become the center for the publication of Catholic liturgical and devotional materials. That city's role as episcopal see, of course, gave the impetus to such printing.

The "Manual" Approach

One of the most popular devotional prayer books among English Catholics which found its way to this country was the *Manual of Devout Prayers* published by Henry Hillis in 1688, most probably in London. It is a work of some interest because of the piety recommended during "assistance at Mass." As we shall see in later books of similar purpose, the *Manual of Devout Prayers* instructed Catholics to assist at Mass devoutly, following along with the priest in Latin, while reading either devotional prayers composed to "unveil" the meaning of the various parts of the Eucharistic liturgy, or reading the very texts of the Mass in English translation as the priest recited them in Latin. However, such an approach to the Eucharist did not mean total non-verbal participation. Devotional-liturgical prayers were also recommended in the *Manual*; e.g., a "Litany of Intercession for England," a series of discreet petitions included among the many vernacular "Prayers for Sunday." English Catholic congregations, led by the priest, prayed for the "reconversion" of England, constantly repeating refrains such as "Have mercy on England," or "Pray for England." Modeled on the Litany of the Saints, the intercessory litany for England addressed the Lord, Mary, the patron saints of England, Scotland, Wales, and Ireland (George, Andrew, David, and Patrick) and other saints popular in the seventeenth century.

Catholic concern for the Church in England was, of course, transplanted to America where the *Manual of Devout Prayers* found a use in the liturgy by lay people in the Maryland colony,[9] although this particular form of prayer for England fell into disuse in the eighteenth century, when sentiment against the "Mother Country" burgeoned.

9. This is rather a tentative conclusion, since I know of only one copy (in the Rare Books and Special Collection section of the Mullen Library at The Catholic University of America) which *seems* to have belonged to an early Catholic settler of the Maryland colony.

The most influential of all eighteenth-century devotional-liturgical books was, perhaps, *The Garden of the Soul; a Manual of Fervent Prayers, Pious Reflections and Solid Instructions*, first composed, edited, and printed by Bishop Challoner around 1740 in London.[10] Challoner was later to be Vicar Apostolic of the London District and all its colonies from 1758 to 1781. Challoner's *Garden of the Soul*, the first American imprint of which was probably published in 1773 in Philadelphia, was widely diffused in the American Catholic settlements and became the model for later devotional works published in the newly independent United States. Besides popular devotions typical of the eighteenth century, *The Garden of the Soul* also contained "Instructions" for the "devout hearing" of and "assistance at Mass," prayers to be said silently by the congregation during Mass, English translations of the Ordinary and the propers of the Mass, and aids for observing Sunday at home. *The Garden of the Soul* also included in its pages Sunday vespers and Benediction, together with instructions on the manner of celebrating and participating in this obligatory Sunday observance.

Between the publication of the anonymous *Manual of Devout Prayers* in 1688 and Challoner's work, other similarly helpful books had been published in England (and later republished or reedited or both in America). These insisted on a specifically liturgical attitude toward Sunday. For example, *Instructions and Devotions for Hearing Mass*, anonymously authored by John Gother (d. 1704) and published posthumously in 1725, demonstrated that Sunday was "made holy"

10. On Challoner's career and writings, see E. H. Burton, *The Life and Times of Bishop Challoner, 1691–1781*, 2 vols. (London, 1909). Challoner's *Garden of the Soul* was not unlike similar Anglican prayerbooks. Cf. R. Russel's *The Devout Christian's Daily Companion and Exercise in Devotion, Containing a Posie of Prayers for Every Day in the Week, and several Occasions; for Families and Private Persons Alone* (London, 1717). Anglican and Catholic spirituality, after all, shared a common medieval liturgical-spiritual tradition in many ways unaffected by the Reformation (or Counter-Reformation).

through participation at Sunday Mass, vespers and Benediction, and through the devout use of various prayers, litanies, and intercessions to Jesus, Mary, and the saints at home by the Catholic family.

One further English work needs to be cited here: that is Alban Butler's work on the liturgical year, *The Moveable Feasts, Fasts and Other Annual Observances of the Catholic Church*. Published posthumously in London in 1774, it was often reprinted through the first half of the nineteenth century in America. Butler's historical-liturgical explanations of Sundays and feasts of the liturgical year profoundly shaped the liturgical understanding of many American Catholics in the period just after the War of Independence.

A positive appreciation of Sunday and the liturgical year, influenced by Alban Butler, can be found in one of the earliest *American* devotional works (i.e., American in authorship and printing): *A Manual of Catholic Prayers*, anonymously authored by the activist pastor of St. Joseph's Church in Philadelphia, Robert Molyneux. Like Challoner's *The Garden of the Soul*, Molyneux's book was for use during the liturgy as well as at home in private prayer.

Two other works of some importance in the shaping of the Anglo-American Catholic's attitude toward the liturgy were the 1792 Georgetown publication *The Pious Guide to Prayer and Devotion* and the *Roman Catholic Manual, or Collection of Prayers, Anthems, Hymns, &c.*, published in Baltimore at the turn of the century. Both books not only influenced devotional life, as Chinnici notes,[11] but also shaped a liturgical mentality that was to last until at least the 1840s, when the first great wave of Irish immigration began.

Before moving on to the actual "look" of Sunday, one must also take note of publications dealing with liturgical music. Several studies have appeared which deal extensively with

11. Cf. n. 3 above.

Catholic hymnody and liturgical music in the late eighteenth century.[12] The first compilation of music for Catholics is the collection edited and published by John Aitken in Philadelphia in 1787. *A Compilation of the Litanies and Vesper Hymns and Anthems As They are Sung in the Catholic Church, Adapted to the Voice or Organ* contained eighteen English hymns (eight with German titles), six litanies (five in Latin, one in German), the Mass of the Blessed Trinity, the Requiem Mass, Sunday vespers, and four antiphons of the Blessed Virgin. Aitken's popular compilation was reprinted in 1791 in an expanded edition, and again in a much revised and further enlarged edition in 1814.

Sunday Liturgy and the Synod of 1791

By running through this catalogue of Catholic liturgical-devotional material, I wish to demonstrate the following point. When the National Synod of 1791 discussed and legislated liturgical matters affecting Sundays and feast days, it was against a background of preexisting liturgical practice already a part of Catholic life, so that the legislation was a reflection of the Synod's expectations of what was possible *liturgically* in Catholic parishes and communities then principally centered in Baltimore, Philadelphia, and New York.

Bishop Carroll and the twenty-two priests who assembled with him in Baltimore in 1791 decreed the following with regard to the observance of Sundays and holy days in four statutes, *"De ordinandis divinis officiis, et festorum observatione."* Statute 17 mandated that on Sundays and holy days the *missa cantata* was to be celebrated, where possible; the Litany of

12. Cf. Mary Camilla Verret, *A Preliminary Survey of Roman Catholic Hymnals Published in the United States of America* (Washington, 1964); on Aitken, pp. 14–15. Concern for Catholic hymnody was evident also in the new diocese of Bardstown in Kentucky where many Maryland Catholics had emigrated. Cf. J. B. Daniel, *Catholic Hymn Book* (Bardstown, 1815), and J. B. David, *Collection of Sacred Hymns for the Use in the Catholic Churches in Kentucky* (Bardstown, 1815). A similar collection had been compiled by Manning and Loring in Boston in 1800: *Anthems, Hymns, Etc. Usually Sung at the Catholick Church in Boston.*

the Blessed Virgin was to be sung or recited; the *Asperges* was
to begin the *missa cantata* on Sunday; the sermon at Mass was
obligatory; vespers and Benediction were to be celebrated in
the afternoon; and vernacular hymns were to be used by the
people. This, of course, was the desired pattern for well-
established parishes where there was more than one priest—a
situation which obtained only in Baltimore, Philadelphia,
and Germantown. The same statute required the proclamation of the Gospel in English (or German or French) after
the priest had read it in Latin. Statute 18 was concerned with
parishes where there was only one priest. In this case, after
Mass the priest led the congregation in the recitation of the
Lord's Prayer, the Hail Mary, the Apostles' Creed, and the
Acts of Faith, Hope, and Charity. In *all* parishes the Prayer
for the Civil Authorities, composed by Carroll himself, was
to be recited immediately after the Gospel and before the
sermon.[13]

This pattern of the *missa cantata*, vespers and Benediction,
and the attentive assistance at Mass with prayer books containing the texts of the Mass, was made possible by the publications already available to Anglo-American Catholics in
the late eighteenth century, and would continue to be possible
well into the nineteenth century as a result of these same
publications and new works inspired by them. In other words,
the existence of the devotional-liturgical books and the legislation of the Synod of 1791, reinforced by Bishop Carroll's
1792 Pastoral Letter,[14] demonstrates a "liturgical" approach
to Sunday worship directly inspired by the ongoing liturgical
tradition of English Catholicism, as yet untouched by the

13. *Statuta Synodi Baltimorensis anno 1791 celebratae*, in *Concilia Provincialia
Baltimori habita ab anno 1829 usque ad annum 1849, Editio altera* (Baltimore, 1851)
17–20.
14. Bishop Carroll's 1792 Pastoral Letter may be found in Peter Guilday's
collection *The National Pastorals of the American Hierarchy* (1792–1919) (Washington, 1923) 1–16.

Counter-Reformation piety of the Continent.[15]

Yet there were problems in the young American Church which affected Sunday liturgy. One such difficulty Carroll addressed in his 1792 pastoral was the relationship between support and maintenance of the clergy, on the one hand, and a community's ability to establish any pattern of worship on Sundays, on the other.

> God has made it our duty to join in the solemn rites of sacrifice and prayer, and in receiving the sacraments instituted for our benefit and the improvement of our souls in piety and grace. The administration of these requires men set apart for and consecrated to so sacred a function. . . .

He goes on to explain that priests are ordained through laying-on of hands by the bishop, not merely for church order but especially for the celebration of the Mass and divine offices. In the same vein, Carroll addressed his flock on the need for what we would today call the proper "environment" for Sunday.

> Hence, likewise, churches for the celebration of divine service, and the great Eucharistic sacrifice of the law of grace, are not built at all, or are suffered to fall into decay.
>
> They are without chalices, without the decent and necessary furniture of the altars, without vestments suited to the different services of the Church, in a word, without those sacred utensils, which its ordinances require, and which contribute to impress the mind with a becoming sense of majesty of religion, and conciliate respect for its august ceremonies. Hence, finally, results the great evil, and the source of many disorders, that, by failing to make provision for the

---

15. The shift from a liturgically centered spirituality to an Italianate, rather Baroque form of piety in the United States is somewhat parallel to a similar change which took place in England with the lifting of the Penal Laws in 1850. Adherents of the Oxford Movement, especially those who eventually would become Roman Catholics, were particularly attracted to Italianate piety. Earlier converts, such as Elizabeth Seton, were likewise drawn into its orbit.

necessary support of pastors, and the maintenance of public worship, you fail likewise of fulfilling the obligation of being present at Mass on every Sunday and holiday; you lose the opportunity of receiving necessary and salutary instruction; and finally, an habitual disregard for the sanctification of the Lord's day, and for the exercise of prayer and religion becomes prevalent.[16]

Carroll obviously did not mince words! Nevertheless, his insistence on the interrelationship between worship, its environment, and the celebrants expresses his appreciation of Sunday, the Lord's day, as the source of Christian spirituality.

The Sunday liturgy would be an important theme of Carroll's continuing correspondence. The nascent Church, for decades, would face difficulties relating to the number of clergy, the building and maintaining of churches, and, most especially, the many pressures faced by a Catholic population often misunderstood and suspected by a non-Catholic majority, and therefore subject to influences militating against the preservation of a liturgical spirituality.[17]

III. Cultural Adaptation

Before moving from this period of the Anglo-American Catholic Church, a few words should be said about the practice of Sunday vespers. Sunday vespers was mandated canonically for each Sunday and holy day by the legislation of 1791 and succeeding provincial and plenary councils of the American Church. How was such legislation implemented?

Nearly all the popular manuals contained some form of vespers (and sometimes matins and lauds) which could be used privately or as a participation aid. *The Pious Guide to Prayer*

16. Pastoral Letter of 1792, Guilday, 7–11, *passim*.
17. See, for example, the variant attitudes of Catholics and Protestants over the Sunday-Sabbath "clash" in Ray Allen Billington's *The Protestant Crusade, 1800–1860: A Study of the Origins of American Nativism* (Chicago, 1938) 195, 323.

and Devotion, first published in Georgetown in 1797 and re-edited and expanded in its more influential 1808 edition, contained the necessary psalms, antiphons, and other texts for vespers. Comparison with the Roman Breviary of the time, however, demonstrates that the celebration advocated for Sunday use in *The Pious Guide* and other later works was an *adapted* version for congregational participation. Only later would English-Latin versions of the Office be available for lay congregational use. In 1839, for example, there appeared the version edited by Fr. Charles Ignatius White, *The Secular's Office, or, Appropriate Exercises for Every Day of the Week, Arranged in a Form Similar to that of the Roman Breviary, To which are added, Morning and Evening Prayers, Devotions for the Time of Mass, &c., &c.*[18] This adaptation of the Divine Office had received the approbation of Samuel Eccleston, S.S., archbishop of Baltimore. Here we have one among many instances in which American bishops of the first half of the nineteenth century understood the need for a kind of "cultural adaptation" of the liturgy for Sundays. Similar forms of the Office are found in Challoner's *The Garden of the Soul,* already mentioned, and in an earlier American devotional, "Arranged by a Clergyman," *The Key of Paradise, Opening the Gate to Eternal Salvation,* published in 1804 in Baltimore with the approval of Bishop Carroll. Other adaptations of vespers for use in parishes can be found well into the mid-nineteenth century. *A Manual of Catholic Devotions for the Use of the Faithful, Who Desire to Live Piously and Die Happily* and *The Ursuline Manual,* first published in London in 1824, revised under the supervision of Bishop John England of Charleston in 1835 and published in Baltimore in 1841, are two examples of this approach.

While the Mass was never "adapted" before the Second Plenary Council of Baltimore in 1866 commissioned a Ceremonial, other rites besides the Office were affected by the

18. Baltimore, 1839.

desires of American bishops to make Sunday and feastday liturgy more "American." One example might be mentioned. Published in Dublin in 1827, *The Office of Holy Week, According to the Roman Missal and Breviary* seemed to have been used extensively in the United States. Its aim was to bring about greater participation in the Holy Week liturgies.

Departure from usual Catholic hymnody also testifies to a liturgical vitality and concern for adaptation in the United States. One such example is *Lyra catholica*, a collection of hymns from the Roman Missal and Roman Breviary, but also (startlingly) from the Breviaries of Cluny and Paris, together with hymns from Italian sources.[19] James L. Meagher's *The Festal Year*, published in 1885, continued this tradition of borrowing from eclectic liturgical sources.

Catholic vernacular hymnody in America was actively encouraged by America's first bishop. By early nineteenth-century standards, the catalogue of collections of hymns and hymn books published in Baltimore, Philadelphia, and Boston with the approbation of Bishop Carroll is long.[20] From 1800 onward, hymnals were increasingly edited for a number of regions ranging from Baltimore to Boston to Bardstown in Kentucky. In general, these early Catholic hymnals contained a majority of English-language hymns plus a few Latin hymns, English anthems and motets, solo organ music, part Masses, and full settings of Sunday and holy day vespers.

Perhaps the most influential liturgical work of the nineteenth century was Bishop John England's *The Roman Missal, Translated into the English Language For the Use of the Laity* (1822),

---

19. The "liturgical orientation" of this work is hinted at from its complete title, *Lyra Catholica: Containing All the Hymns of the Roman Breviary and Missal, With Others from Various Sources. Arranged for Every Day in the Week, and the Festivals and Saints' Days Throughout the Year. With a Selection of Hymns, Anthems, and Sacred Poetry, From Approved Sources* (New York, 1851). *Lyra Catholica* was originally compiled by Edward Caswall, a convert from the Church of England, who published the collections in London in 1849.

20. Cf. Verret, n. 12 above.

a book also containing Sunday vespers.[21] The Bishop of Charleston had gotten into trouble both with Archbishop Ambrose Maréchal of Baltimore and the Congregation for the Propagation of the Faith in Rome over the Missal's publication, for it was a *complete* translation into English of all the liturgical texts of the *Missale Romanum*—something not permitted at the time. Bishop England's Missal was, in fact, of Irish origin and had been in use in Ireland for years in the early eighteenth century. The bishop's publication altered the course of liturgical participation on Sundays in the sense that, with all the texts now in front of them, lay people could "follow along with the priest," a mode of participation at Sunday liturgy which would last until the vernacularization of the Roman Rite in this century.

Other Vernaculars

For many years after Independence, the Anglo-American Catholic Church was the dominant strand of American Catholicism, not indeed because of numbers (especially when one remembers that most of America's territories consisted of land formerly held by Spain and France for centuries), but because Church authority was focused in the old Maryland mission of the Jesuits and held by the Anglo-Irish and English Catholic families who fled the mother country in the seventeenth century. Carroll was from such a family, and many of the American priests of his time, few as they

---

21. Bishop England's *Roman Missal* deserves a separate study of its own. The forerunner in many ways of the American liturgical movement's preoccupation with people's missals, England's hand-missal began a popular liturgical tradition which antedates European efforts to produce such participatory aids. Gueranger could not later "get away" with what England championed: the entire Mass available *in English* to th person in the pew. The bishop of Charleston did not get off scot-free for his efforts. Cf. Peter Guilday, *The Life and Times of John England, First Bishop of Charleston (1786–1842),* 2 vols. (New York, 1927) I:330–333; and Francis J. Weber, "America's First Vernacular Missal," *America's Catholic Heritage, Some Bicentennial Reflections (1776–1976)* (St. Paul Editions, 1976) 31–33.

were, also hailed from such families. Besides, the new United
States of America was "*English* America" in the consciousness
of the newly-independent states.

Nevertheless, Catholicism had already been implanted
within the territorial limits of the United States in Carroll's
time by the French and Spanish before the Maryland mission
came into existence. Moreover, it must be remembered that
migration of German Catholics to Pennsylvania in the early
eighteenth century brought to the American Church, even
before its first bishop was ordained, a wholly different strand
of Catholic liturgical piety. Thus, there were "other vernaculars" shaping Sunday worship.

Vernacular in the liturgy was also important to the French
Catholics of the United States and influenced Sunday worship
among them. The arrival of the Sulpicians in Baltimore gave
the Church its own seminary in 1791 and a supply of sem-
inarians and priests to send to the "hinterlands" of America—
Indiana and Michigan—there to minister to French Catholics.
In 1798 *Cantiques français a l'usage du Catéchisme de l'Église de Saint-
Patrice de Baltimore* was published in that city for use both in the
liturgy and in catechism classes for children. This collection of
French liturgical and devotional hymns was used also in other
parts of the country. Also worth mentioning is the bilingual
(French-English) *Epistles and Gospels for Sundays and Holidays
Throughout the Year*, published in Detroit in 1812 by Gabriel
Richard, a Sulpician missionary. The history of this liturgical
book is itself interesting. In Michigan, under the French, *both*
the Epistle and the Gospel were read in the vernacular at
Sunday Mass, whereas only the Gospel was read in English
in the thirteen original states.

IV. IMMIGRATION AND NEW IDEAS

The brief sketch outlined above touches on only a few of the
liturgical-devotional works which Anglo-American Catholics

had at their disposal in the pew or in their homes. A good deal more research must be done before any firm conclusions can be drawn. As already mentioned, there were other vernaculars of some significance in the American Church. I have alluded only to French and German in a fleeting way. America's territories, however, encompassed significant numbers of Spanish-speaking Catholics who also were under the jurisdiction of the archbishop of Baltimore, and later of southern and western ecclesiastical districts. These, too, played a role, albeit a marginal one, in the life of the early Anglo-American Church of the United States. Limitations of space prevent anything more than a mention of this aspect of "Catholic Sunday in America."

What emerges from the above considerations thus far is the following: the use of the vernacular by Anglo-, French-, and German-American Catholics was firmly established and widespread well into the middle of the nineteenth century. At that point, American Catholicism's isolation began to lessen, as immigration of non-English-speaking Catholics from southern and central Europe considerably increased. Immigration not only swelled the *numbers* of Catholics but also initiated an ineluctable change in the *patterns* of piety and Sunday worship. European emigrés brought with them their ideas, their customs, their spiritualities, their devotions; and these, from continental Europe, were largely of a Counter-Reformation type, hitherto largely unknown in the United States. The same struggle between pre-Reformation English piety (of a liturgical type) and Counter-Reformation and ultramontane spirituality would also characterize English Catholicism as it moved out from under the yoke of the Penal Laws.

Hard on the heels of Catholic immigration came the Nativist reaction, a response which caused Catholics to retreat further into a new-found individualist ghetto-piety—a piety which would eventually evolve into the fully developed "for-God-and-country" Catholic style of life, ideology, and mores.

Not only could one be a Catholic and an American; some believed it was possible to be more American if one were a Catholic. The conciliar epoch of this century would change all that.

V. The "Catholic Sabbath"

Finally, there is one other significant factor that would change the Catholic experience of Sunday in America—a new-found sabbatarianism, foreign to English Catholicism but endemic to American forms of Christianity. While "servile work" was forbidden to Catholics on Sundays and holy days, the New England Puritan legacy broadened the Roman Catholic definition of *opus servile* to exclude even the most innocent divertissements on the Lord's Day. The introduction of Irish Jansenism, French Gallicanism, and Italian Baroque piety merely reinforced the Puritan ideal of Sunday. Catholics would become just as virulently opposed to the sale of "demon rum" in most states as were their Protestant brothers and sisters. Catholic bishops would lobby just as hard for "blue laws" as did the most popular circuit preachers and evangelists. In the end, Sunday would resemble for American Catholics the Sunday forged by Protestant Yankees since the sixteenth century. Liturgical piety, a liturgical spirituality precious to America's first English Catholics, and a "liturgical" Sunday would all imperceptibly disappear into that version of Sunday against which the twentieth-century liturgical movement struggled.

If there is any conclusion to be drawn from these tentative reflections, it is this: until the middle of the nineteenth century, American Catholicism, like its original source (English Catholicism), knew a liturgical piety and spirituality which shaped the average Catholic's understanding of the nature and meaning of Sunday. As seen from the few liturgical-devotional works we have examined, this seems to be the case. Furthermore, the shift in meaning seems to have come about with the introduction of a Counter-Reformation spirituality when European immigration was on the rise. Coupled with a new-found "Americanism," one of the principal pillars of which was a fundamental sabbatarianism, "Catholic Sunday in America" came to be a spiritual expression several times removed from true liturgical piety, ultimately necessitating, as Ahlstrom and others have pointed out, the sweeping reforms advocated by the American liturgical movement.

The Role of Sunday in American Society: Has It Changed?

WILLIAM C. MCCREADY

To a considerable extent, the remarks that follow are an exercise in what anthropologists call "thick description." Essentially this means looking at social activities and weaving interpretation in between our understanding of the details of the activity, rather than leaving interpretation until later when we are back in our study and analyzing our notes. Gilbert Ryle's description of several young boys winking at each other contains the seeds of understanding this methodology.[1] "Thin description" would be that the actor is "rapidly contracting his right eyelid," while "thick description" would be that the actor was "practicing a burlesque of a friend faking a wink to deceive an innocent into thinking a conspiracy is in motion."

1. Gilbert Ryle, *The Concept of Mind* (New York: Barnes & Noble, 1969).

WILLIAM MCCREADY holds a Ph.D in sociology from the University of Illinois and has served on the staff of the National Opinion Research Center at the University of Chicago since 1971. He is currently director of the university's Cultural Pluralism Research Center and associate professor in the school of social service administration. He is a member of the U.S.C.C. Commission on Marriage and Family Life.

This technique is required in order to penetrate and understand culture and the meanings which it carries for us. To quote Clifford Geertz:

> Culture is public because meaning is. You can't wink (or burlesque one) without knowing what counts as winking or how, physically, to contract your eyelids, and you can't conduct a sheep raid (or mimic one) without knowing what it is to steal a sheep and how practically to go about it. But to draw from such truths the conclusion that knowing how to wink is winking and knowing how to steal sheep is sheep raiding is to betray as deep a confusion as, taking thin descriptions for thick, to identify winking with eyelid contractions or sheep raiding with chasing wooly animals out of pastures.[2]

In another brilliant ethnographic venture, Walker Percy discusses the Bororo man who says he is a parakeet. Rather than dismiss the man as being totemistic, the ethnographer proceeds to weave together into one narrative his perception and understanding of what is before him:

> A man who says he is a parakeet is, if he says it in normal conversation, saying that, as myth and ritual demonstrate, he is shot through with parakeetness and that this religious fact has some crucial social implications—we parakeets must stick together, not marry one another, not eat mundane parakeets, and so on, for to do otherwise is to act against the grain of the whole universe.[3]

According to this paradigm, the moods and motivations induced by religious practice appear to the individual to be sensible: the only way to act, given the way things really are.

This is the key to understanding religious activity in the social context. The purpose of myth is to articulate the way things really are: to convey the sense of underlying order in the society and the culture without the need for detailed

2. Clifford Geertz, The Interpretation of Cultures (New York: Basic Books, 1973) 12.

3. Walker Percy, "The Symbolic Structure of Interpersonal Process," Psychiatry, XXIV (1961) 39–52.

and parsimonious articulation, but through actions which are filled with meanings and flexible sensitivities, and which can only be analyzed using "thick description." This is the way I will try to approach our discussion of the role of Sunday in our contemporary society.

Sunday is a mythic day. From a sociocultural point of view, this means that Sunday is not only a day but also a social fact which contains meanings and subjective realities which both reflect and create changes in our society. Sunday not only breaks time up into weeks but it is also a day on which we summarize things and wrap them up and take stock of how far we've come. Is this all a product of our imagination because we are gathered for a conference about Sundays, or does it really happen? Do people really treat Sundays differently in the way they perceive the use of time? That will be the major point of my remarks today.

First, we will consider the question of the mythic qualities of Sundays. We will look at the questions of the deep myth and the midrange myth, and we will use these conceptualizations to direct our examination of subsequent data. Second, by looking at some surveys, we will explore how people use their time on Sundays. Third, we will concentrate on the religious dimensions of Sunday, both in terms of devotional practice and in terms of people's attitudes (particularly Catholics) towards the liturgy and towards liturgical changes. Fourth, we will turn our attention to the different perspectives which clergy and lay people have about this time of the week and see whether that enlightens our understanding of the sacred day. Fifth, we will cover the different impact and meanings that Sunday has for young people, middle-aged people, and old people. In other words, we will look at the life-cycle dimensions of Sunday. In the final section, we will discuss certain implications which the data and research and sociologizing has for our study of the use of Sundays.

I. The Social Myth

There are special events in human life which have the quality of encapsulating and summarizing the forces and influences and characteristics of more than just the immediate present. These are mythic events. They are the sociologists' version of sacraments: signs which carry meaning beyond the simple meaning of the event itself. Sunday can be considered such an event. The day carries many levels of meanings and probably for most people different levels of memory as well. One Sunday brings to mind other Sundays and other meaningful events. We use it as a marker of the passage of time. We use it as an occasion to celebrate and an occasion to worship. Although some denominations worship on other days of the week, the civil religion that is American calls Sunday its own. For at least a few moments, we will try to delineate the mythic elements of Sunday, and for purposes of clarity I have tried to separate them into two groups: the midrange myth, that which is closer to the surface; and the deep myth, that which lies underneath all else.

The midrange of mythical experience is made up of those characteristics which describe rather than define reality. In other words, it is a set of characteristics which are detailed descriptions or, perhaps, in Clifford Geertz's words, "thick descriptions," yet are not as definitional as the latter stages of the deep myth. The kinds of characteristics which describe Sunday are the following.

Sunday is a day for relaxing and a day when few demands are made. Now, any man who has had plans to go to a ballgame or just to sit and enjoy himself and then has his wife come along and tell him there are jobs to be done or that there are kids to be taken somewhere knows that Sunday is not a day without demands. However, it is a day when the usual demands of the work place, of the profession, of the career, of the employing institution, are held in suspension. This characteristic of relaxation and the absence of customary demands makes Sunday a special place, a special time. It's a private time, a time for personal matters, a time of our own. It may be the only day of the week that we own, in the sense of having the freedom to consume it pretty much as we wish.

Sunday is also a time which reveals in a special way the power structure and differentiation within the family. Sunday is different for men and women. The point made earlier about relaxing and making it our own day is to a considerable extent a male point of view because, if anything, women tend to work more on Sunday. This is likely to become more important in the future as we have more two-career families with the men tending to consider Sunday a day off, whereas the women not only have their career or job during the week, but they do not have a particular day off on Sunday. Sunday makes the separation dramatically clear because both parties are at home, so that, whether or not the woman works during the week, the contrast between the male behavior and the female behavior on this "day off" is made pointedly clear on this one day. This contrast makes Sunday a day of tension in many families, as well as a day of relaxation, compounding the mythic nature of the day.

Sunday is a universal day of worship. Since Sunday is the day when most people go to church, it can be considered to be the "blessed day" in our culture. We will come back to examine this characteristic in several sections of the paper, but for the moment it is enough to say that this characteristic adds a certain sacred or sacramental dimension to this particular day. As mentioned earlier, this is true not only of denominational religion but also of the civil religion which is a theme within American society. We honor our various civil religious celebrations on this day as well: celebrations such as public events, political events, sports events, various cultural expressions of our unity and our purpose.

Sunday is a day for families to spend together. This statement begins to bridge the midrange myth and the deep myth. Sunday is a day when parents and children and grandparents visit each other, spend time with each other, do special things with each other. It is a time for trips to grandma's house, trips to the zoo, going to or participating in various sporting events together, and going outdoors. At the midrange level, this is a descriptive phenomenon of the unity of the family, and it also accentuates the sense of unity that families have with each other. It helps us reinforce our notion that our primary group is an important national resource and characteristic and that we engage in little mini-celebrations of family on this one day of the week. Obviously these celebrations are not always without tension, but that adds to the credibility of the description and the credibility of the day as being special.

The deep-myth characteristics are a bit more difficult to describe because they lie considerably beneath the surface of the rational and conscious parts of our intellect and are involved more with the primordial and preconscious parts of our personality. The first characteristic that is connected to the deep myth of Sundays is its designation as a day for family and for children. The first characteristic of the deep myth, in other words, is that of *regeneration*.

Sunday is a time not only for relaxing but also for literally regenerating our culture. It is a time for reminding ourselves that we have children to care for and that we have a history to celebrate. Every so often special Sundays come along which combine both of those and tend to become truly memorable experiences. The regeneration myth is closely connected to our need to know where we come from, who we are, and where we are going. It helps put us in a context of history and of other generations, and we use a variety of symbols— children, nostalgia, family memories, scrapbooks—and a variety of other stimuli to remind us that we are a part of a human chain that extends back into history and forward into the future. There is a mystical quality of being a part of all that has lived and all that will live which seems to be available to us in these moments of reflecting on the regenerative properties of our culture. Sunday seems to be a unique time when those symbols are available to us.

A second property of the deep myth is a *pride in achievement* which we celebrate on Sundays. Sunday is not only a time for relaxation in the sense of time off but also a time for looking back on what we have achieved and taking some enjoyment in it. A sense of achievement is part of the deep myth because it reflects our dominance over nature and our ability to survive from one era to the next. Achievement is a sign of the human characteristic of continuing adaptability which is at the very core of who we are. Of course, it is possible to corrupt all of these things. The heightened sense of competition which we see in spectator sports, which are so common on Sunday, could be read as a negative influence and a preoccupation with winning. However, I believe that the mirror image of those preoccupations is the deep myth of achieving mastery over one's environment and successfully adapting to it so that succeeding generations are in fact possible. Sunday becomes the celebration of the continuation of life and the celebration of the triumph over obstacles at least for one more week.

Finally, the third characteristic of the deep myth is that *we deserve a rest on Sunday because we have worked hard.* Hard labor is the flip-side of achievement. Not only is Sunday a time for looking back on achievements, but it is a time for justice, for getting what we deserve, for getting what we have earned. It is a time for celebrating the justice there is in the cosmic plan or in God's world. We in fact do get a day of rest and a day to enjoy ourselves and a day to let our minds wander into the future and let our dreams become reality. That's what deserving a rest is all about; it's not a breathing stop on a marathon race. The element of *deserving* the rest is important as well because it reflects on the worthwhileness and importance of our individual personhood. It is not that society deserves rest, but that *we* deserve it.

These two large dimensions of the cultural experience of Sunday, the midrange myth and the deep myth, are the context within which we will now discuss the changing uses of Sunday and the way in which people's time has been spent over the years. One of the difficult things to do in this context is to decide whether changes are large or small and whether they are important or unimportant. Initially, we are simply going to present some data about the way people view Sundays in both a secular and a religious sense and the way in which those uses have changed over the last several decades.

II. Research Regarding the Use of Time

The 1975–76 University of Michigan Time-Use Study provides us with a glimpse of how people use time according to different days of the week and different activities.[4] These data will give us an insight into how people use their time right now, but there really is no comparable data going back ten or twenty or thirty years; therefore, we will have to make some judicious speculations about what kinds of changes there have been. (There is a simpler set of data from 1965, and we will refer to that later, but it is not as rich as the current one.)

In Table 1, thirteen categories of activity account for about 90 percent of the time spent on an average weekday, a Saturday, or a Sunday, but the categories differ from day to day.

---

4. Juster and Stafford, *Essays in the Use of Time Among American Households* (Manuscript copy, 1980). There were 1519 respondents with at least one data point, 975 with at least three, and 873 with all four data points. The principal data collection was done with a diary.

TABLE 1

Time Spent on Activities by Day of Week
(In Minutes)

	Weekdays	Saturday	Sunday
Sleep	469	498	528
Work	287	98	56
Meals[1]	128	142	144
Household chores	127	160	125
TV viewing	113	118	150
Shopping	50	64	22
Visiting	33	57	70
Reading	30	31	48
Sports and hobbies	28	47	48
Naps	22	30	28
Telephone conversation	19	15	15
Cultural activities[2]	15	31	26
Religious activities[3]	8	10	42
Total	1,309	1,301	1,302
Percent of day accounted for	91%	90%	90%

SOURCE: University of Michigan Time-Use Study, 1975–76.

[1]Includes eating, preparation, and cleaning up.
[2]Includes movies, theater, musical events, and other special activities.
[3]Includes church attendance, choir attendance, etc.

Obviously, the thing that we spend the most time on, on all of these days, is sleeping; and we sleep about an hour more on Sundays than we do on Saturdays or weekdays. The thing that we do next most often on the weekdays is go to work, and on Saturdays we tend to do household chores, and on Sundays we watch television. The activity that takes third

place on each of the days is eating or preparing food or cleaning up after we have eaten. The activity that takes fourth
place on a weekday is household chores, and number four
on Saturdays is watching television, and then we are back
to household chores again for our fourth-place activity on
Sundays. Television drops to fifth place for weekdays, while
work comes in fifth on Saturday, and visiting or socializing
with our friends and relatives comes in fifth on Sundays. The
sixth-place activity during the week is shopping, and the
same is true for Saturdays, while the sixth-place activity for
Sundays is working. The seventh-place activity for both
weekdays and Saturdays is visiting, and for Sunday, sports
and hobbies and reading tie for seventh place. In the eighth

TABLE 2

Percentage of Non-Sleep Time Spent on Activities

	Weekdays	Saturday	Sunday
Work	34	13	7
Meals	15	18	20
Household chores	15	21	17
TV viewing	14	15	21
Shopping	6	8	2
Visiting	4	7	9
Reading	4	4	6
Sports and hobbies	3	6	6
Telephone conversation	2	2	2
Cultural activities	2	4	3
Religious activities	1	1	6
Total	100	99*	99*

SOURCE: University of Michigan Time-Use Study, 1975-76.

* Due to rounding error.

place, the activity for weekdays is reading, for Saturdays it's sports and hobbies, and for Sundays it's religion.

Another way to characterize each of these kinds of days is to look at the proportion of non-sleep time that is spent on various activities for various days. These data are presented in Table 2. Two-thirds of our non-sleep time on weekdays is taken up by working, something to do with meals, or doing chores around the house. These same activities occupy a little more than half of our time on a Saturday and a little less than half of our time on a Sunday. The single category which most characterizes our activity on Sundays is watching television. We do spend proportionately more time on religion on Sundays and a bit more time on things to do with meals.

TABLE 3

PERCENTAGE OF RESPONDENTS IN A WASHINGTON DC STUDY (1969)
ENGAGED IN VARIOUS ACTIVITIES BY DAY OF WEEK

	Weekdays	Saturday	Sunday
Sleep	99	99	99
Meals	96	90	90
Personal care	84	72	76
Travel	83	74	67
TV viewing	67	60	67
Household chores and child care	66	67	62
Work	58	18	12
Shopping	36	48	15
Religious activities	4	5	32
Reading	46	33	58

SOURCE: F. S. Chapin, *Human Activity Patterns in the City* (New York: Wiley-Interscience, 1974) 253–55.

We can get still another perspective on how we use Sundays as contrasted with other days by looking at the proportion of the population engaged in certain activities by the day of the week. In Table 3 these data are presented for the Washington, D.C., metropolitan area, and some clear differences between days emerge. The proportion of people working declines dramatically on the weekends, and the proportion shopping is very much lower on Sunday than on Saturday. Religious activity is certainly higher on Sunday, as is the proportion of the sample engaged in reading. Rather than intensity or amount of time devoted to various activities, these data indicate simple incidence, which gives us a slightly better view of the activities which the majority of people view as appropriate for various days. The central finding in this table is the dramatic decline in the use of Sunday as a shopping day when contrasted with Saturday. How would we summarize these three tables?

It is safe to say that Sunday has not become secularized in the sense that we either work or go shopping to an extraordinary degree. As a matter of fact, the proportion of time spent on both those activities goes down rather dramatically on this particular day. The proportion of time devoted to religion is appropriately high compared to the other days of the week, and time devoted to family activities, particularly to eating meals, is also higher. Sunday has become a popular day for watching television and for engaging in other recreational activities, all of which goes along with the idea that it is a day of rest and a special day within the week. There is ample evidence in these data to indicate that Sunday is still considered a special day.

In the analysis of the Michigan data that has been done by other sociologists, a couple of interesting points are made. For example, Martha Hill, in chapter 4, quotes the following:

American adults spend about the same amount of time in organizational activity including religion as they did in child care. A breakdown of organizational activity according to the title of organization indicates that religious practice (attending services, singing in the choir and praying) was the dominant form of organizational time commitment.[5]

Later in the same chapter, Hill notes:

> The major aspect in which Sundays differ from other days is the time devoted to organizations: about three times as much is spent Sunday on organizations, with religious practice being the predominant activity with increased time allotments.[6]

In another report documenting the changes in Americans' use of time between 1965 and 1975, John Robinson notes:

> While increases in sleep and other personal care suggest a more relaxed lifestyle in 1975, the data on free time are far more persuasive in this regard. The overall ten percent increase in free time over 1965 is shared by all six population groups. However, certain groups seem to have gained more free time than others; namely, single employed men, married employed women, and single housewives.[7]

Robinson also points out that between 1965 and 1975 the amount of time devoted to organizational activity increased for all of these groups and, as we have already seen, the predominant form of organizational activity is religious.

In another article by John Robinson entitled "Television and Leisure Time: A New Tomorrow?" the author points out that religion was one of the activities to gain in minutes per day allocated to it between 1965 and 1975.[8] The major categories which gained time allocations between 1965 and 1975 were sleeping, studying, religion, hobbies, television watching, and magazine reading. Again, these data seem to indicate that there has been an increase rather than a decrease

---

5. *Ibid.*, ch. 4, 10.
6. *Ibid.*, ch. 4, 33.
7. *Ibid.*, ch. 6, no page reference, subhead RESULTS.
8. *Ibid.*, ch. 10, Table 2, p. 7.

in time allocated to religious activities during the last fifteen years or so.

These studies give us a context for seeing the way we use time currently and at least a hint as to what the context was ten years ago. Additional data which go back a few years further will allow us to examine the specifically religious nature of Sunday.

III. RELIGIOUS BEHAVIOR

There are two kinds of data available about religious practices or religious behavior on Sundays: figures about the actual attendance at church and data about the attitudes people have regarding their liturgies and the quality of them. Church attendance figures differ for Protestants and for Catholics over the last twenty years in the following way. Between 1957 and now, there has been a maximum swing for Protestants of about 7 percent.[9] Protestant church attendance reached a high in 1957 of 44 percent weekly attendance and a low in the mid-seventies of 37 percent. It is now back up to 40 percent. Catholic church attendance, on the other hand, has a maximum swing between 1957 and 1981 of over 20 percent with a high of 75 percent attending church every week in 1957 to a low of 54 percent in 1975, and now moving back up to the 55 and 65 percent range.[10] The major point to remember here is that the decline in church attendance is to a very great extent a specifically Catholic phenomenon and is not a sign of a general secularization of society. The implication for our current concern is that Sundays are still a very religious day even though Catholic churches have

9. Carroll, Johnson, and Marty, *Religion in America: 1950 to the Present* (New York: Harper & Row, 1979) 18–22.

10. Greeley, McCready, and McCourt, *Catholic Schools in a Declining Church* (Kansas City: Sheed & Ward, 1976) 120.

suffered some serious setbacks in terms of the proportion of people attending Mass.

A word is in order about the interpretation of this decline in attendance since it is always a controversial subject. Our research has provided a convergence of findings which support the contention that the encyclical *Humanae Vitae* was a strategic mistake, coming along as it did in the midst of a previously changed contraceptive behavior among Catholic women and disappointing the expectations that there would be a relaxation of the rules. Other possible explanations of the decline, such as dissatisfaction with liturgical changes or a dissatisfaction with the social justice positions of the Church, have been tested with data adequate to the job and have not been supported. One of the reasons that the declines were not immediately apparent to the people in the pulpit was that the Catholic population had grown sufficiently to continue to fill up the existing churches so that the absent members were not sorely missed. That is now changing, and the decline in church attendance together with the lower birth rate is resulting in more vacant pews and is beginning to be noticed more frequently by clerical observers.

There are also several attitudinal changes regarding the Sunday activities which are important for our consideration.[11] The first attitude has to do with the overall approval of the liturgical changes within the Church. While there is certainly a sense that if people want to have traditional Masses, they ought to be allowed to do so, there is also a strong approval of the Mass in English and the introduction of non-traditional musical styles and other liturgical innovations, which belies the conventional wisdom that people are unhappy with their liturgical experiences. People may be un-

---

11. *Ibid.*, 110–115 and William McCready, *Changing Attitudes of American Catholics Towards the Liturgy* (Federation of Diocesan Liturgical Commissions, 1974).

happy with the interpretations which liturgy committees and directors of liturgical art place on their behavior, but they do not appear to be unhappy with liturgical experiences.

A second point is that over the last ten or fifteen years, people's reason for attending Mass has shifted from a fear of committing a sin to a desire to express worship. Back in 1964 most people felt it was a sin to miss Mass, and that fact was a major reason for their attendance. In more recent times, they have been more reluctant to say that it is a sin to miss Mass, and they are more likely to say that the reason they go to Mass is to worship God. These data seem to be inconsistent with the notion that Sunday is less religious than it used to be, or that people are taking their religious observances less seriously; if anything, they seem to indicate that they are taking them more seriously.

Finally, we have asked questions about people's attitudes towards the quality of sermons over the last fifteen years and have found a significant decline in the rating which people assign the Sunday sermon. The proportion of the population saying that a sermon was excellent has dropped from approximately 44 percent in the mid-sixties to approximately 20 percent in the current period. It is worth noting that this decline of the excellent rating of sermons does not accompany a decline in respect for the priesthood, nor does it accompany a decline in the opinion that the priests are doing a good job. By and large, people still give priests high marks for being concerned and for being empathetic and sensitive; they simply do not think they give sermons the way they used to.

IV. CONTRASTING PERSPECTIVES ON SUNDAY: CLERGY AND PEOPLE

One of the perplexing problems in trying to deal with the Christian community and the Catholic parish and its attitude and perspective towards the use of Sundays is that two important elements of the social structure, the clergy and the laity, have very different views of the day. For the laity, it's a day off and a day of relaxation, and to some extent it involves their religious observance. For the clergy, it's their primary work day, one on which they have duties that are very public and important. This is not to demean or to limit the ministry that goes on during the week, but there is no question that for the clergy what happens on Sunday is a crucial element in their professional identity. How do these two contrasting styles of thought fit together?

The real problem is one of "non-congruent" expectations. The clergy, since they view Sunday as their work day and the primary religious celebration in the parish, expect that the laity will also view this as a primary celebration of their faith. The laity, on the other hand, may be viewing the Sunday celebration as quite a different thing. It may be simply the initial step in a day of relaxation which has not only been particularly religious but has also had the deep mythical qualities which we addressed in the first section of the paper. If this scenario is true, then several things follow.

Priests are going to be disappointed in the laity and in the way the laity celebrate the liturgy because they really expect the laity to focus some sort of culmination of their community faith on the Sunday celebration. The laity, on the other hand, are going to be disappointed because they see this as the time for the priest to shine and to give them leadership and vision, to speak clearly about religion in their lives; yet, at least according to their evaluation of the sermons, that's not what they seem to be getting. What I am trying to point to here is that the malaise that we see in parishes surrounding the Sunday liturgy may not be a malaise due to the quality of the liturgy or the secularization of society, but rather to the mutually divergent expectations of the clergy and laity about each other's appropriate behavior. The rethinking of this matter is a burden which falls more heavily on the clergy than on the laity at this stage of the game because the clergy must come to redefine and rethink and understand in a new way their role as the official presiders of the faith community, rather than the harried administrators of the parish plant or the all-purpose ministers who are destined to suffer burnout in the near future.

V. Sundays and the Life Cycle

Sundays are perceived differently not only by clergy and laity but also by people at different stages of the life cycle. When I was in grammar school, we had a children's Mass on Sunday to which all of the school children were expected to go, and I guess most did. There was something special about that experience because although we might publicly grouse about it and say what a tedious thing it was (and, especially as we got older, how onerous it was to be lumped with the younger children), I suspect we also felt that we were glad that somebody cared enough about whether we went to church to make us do it. It somehow made it easier that we were there with our peers rather than having to go to church with our families. Sunday celebrations are essentially uncomfortable for most young people, probably because they are run by adults, and adults just don't know how to do celebrations the way young people do. The currently fashionable wisdom says that a parish is a community of faith and that the separate groups within the parish ought not to divide themselves off from the main body and go around worshiping by themselves. I think I understand the theological underpinnings of such an attitude, but the sociology is not very good. It would seem to me that one could do both; have Masses every so often that were by, for, and about young people, that spoke to their religious issues; and at the same time, have Masses where the entire community was welcome. We seem to be locked into thinking that if we have Masses for young people, we have to have them every week, or if we do anything else we have to do it all the time, and that is very dysfunctional. Young people face special religious issues at their stage of life, and those issues need to be voiced in special ways.

People in the middle of their life cycle are usually people who are caring for young people themselves and still perhaps relating to their older parents, while simultaneously going through all of the hectic and disconcerting activity surrounding professional growth, establishment of family, etc. These people are the majority of the parish network, and they probably need good sermons more than anyone else. They come to church with a bit more maturity than the young and without the wisdom and nostalgia of the old, but needing a great deal from the hour that they spend there. Increasingly, according to our data, they feel as though they are not getting the religious attention they need, which is probably partly their own fault and partly the fault of their clergy. People at this stage of the life cycle frequently need to be reminded of the larger religious vision of which they are a part and the heritage from which they come. They need to have their religious sensibilities restored and some perspective and balance put into their lives. High-quality sermons which help them to interpret their own experiences in the light of religious wisdom are perhaps the most beneficial use of this hour that happens every week. For these people, the traditional sermon and the traditional liturgy are extremely important.

For people near the end of the life cycle, a different set of concerns emerge. The major religious issue for people at this stage of life is hope, and the question as to whether it is a worthwhile perspective or not. Hope is a little bit difficult to deliver in a sermon, but it is wonderfully easy to communicate in a party or a celebration. These people need to be made a part of whatever kind of liturgy is going on, and one of the simpler solutions to some of their difficulties is to have the parish provide transportation to get to the church. Older people love to get out of the house, and anything that can make it easier for them to get to the church for a Sunday celebration is probably of immense religious benefit.

It is not only that people at different stages in the life cycle perceive Sundays in different ways, but it is also probably the case that Sundays have to some extent changed over time, not simply from the fifties to the present time, but from the early part of this century to the present time. Unfortunately, we have very little data stretching back that far, but in the final section of this presentation we will try to discuss some of the implications of the present data and speculate about what some of these long-term trends might be.

VI. IMPLICATIONS AND CONCLUSION

One of the first questions to ask about these data and about the role of Sunday in particular is: is it more or less special than in the past? Given the data on time use, it is easy to see that Sunday is in fact still a special day. It has a different time-use pattern and it is not a day like weekdays or even like Saturdays. It is also still a religious day—whether, in fact, it is a more religious or less religious day, we really cannot tell, but it is certainly still a religious day. In some ways, it is misleading and erroneous to compare the present time to the mid-fifties because according to a number of social science studies, the mid-fifties was a very deviant time itself. If we look at demographic patterns, for example, we can see that the trends which we think are so special (that is, single-parent families and increasing divorces and more people living alone) were in fact trends that started back in the twenties and thirties and which took a hiatus during the forties and fifties, and we are now coming back to those patterns. I would not doubt that other kinds of social patterns of value and religion were distorted by the same mechanism. That is to say, if we compare ourselves to the high church-attendance rates and to the high feelings of well-being and peacefulness that were present during the fifties, we may be making the wrong comparison. If, on the other hand, we go back to the early 1900s, a couple of things stand out very clearly.

According to the time-use data, people spend approximately two-and-a-half hours watching the television on Sunday. Now, in the early part of the century, that was impossible because there simply was no television to watch, so what else were they doing? Well, one safe bet is that they were probably doing more activities with other people than they are now. So to some extent the physical interaction between people is probably less now than it was in the early 1900s. It's also possible that reading has declined, although probably not by a great deal. It may well be that in the early 1900s, or at least in the mid-twenties and thirties, radio was as popular as television is now, although again we have relatively little data with which to examine that kind of supposition.

Let us for the moment examine a proposition that there is less physical interaction between people than there used to be. If that is true, and if it is the result of television viewing, it is also true that there is a greater scope of information being presented to people; that is, while they may not be in personal contact with other people, through television they are in contact with people and events they would never have seen in the earlier days. We don't really know what the impact of that widened scope of attention is, but we could surmise that it increases the level of general information and knowledge while decreasing the extent to which experiences are reflected upon. One tends to reflect upon one's own interactions rather than upon experiences which are seen on a videotube to have happened to a third party.

Another question which these data raise is the question of whether we shape Sunday or whether Sunday shapes us. Is Sunday special because we make it that way, or does what happens on Sunday somehow change us? If Sunday is truly a mythic day, then in fact both things happen at the same time. Our activities on Sunday both change our lives and give shape and definition and boundaries to them, and those same activities are also shaped by the fact that they happen on Sunday. They are given a different meaning by happening on that day of the week. In other words, we both *do* special kinds of activities on Sunday and *because* we do those activities Sunday becomes a special day which represents a deeper meaning to us. This factor does not seem to be changing over the course of time; i.e., the evidence would still indicate that Sunday is a unique and special day, containing messages about the meaning of life and perhaps deeper messages about the history and meaning of our own personal lives.

Some people would say that religion ought not to be confined to Sunday and that Sunday does a disservice by providing a catchall for our religious sensibilities. Others would take the point of view that Sunday is very special and sacred and we ought to do everything we can to emphasize that. From a sociological point of view, Sunday is a very special day, and the trick is to learn how to use the specialness of that day to reflect upon the rest of the week. That is, not to make every day like Sunday or to make Sunday like every other day, but rather to take what is special about the Sunday experience and use it to examine the week, to stimulate us for the future, to reflect upon our experiences, and to enter into the deep myth that Sunday represents.

If Sundays have changed dramatically over the course of this century, my suspicion is that they have changed in the following way. In bygone days, when there were fewer multiple demands made on our time by the exigencies of occupation and the way we define our intimate family relationships, Sunday was in fact a day of relaxation, appreciation, and deserved quiet. Increasingly it has become a day for catching up with life's pace. The effect of this is to trivialize Sunday and to make it the "last-minute day" on which we catch up with all the things we didn't get to that week, so that we start the new week with a clean slate. This wastes an important cultural symbol and trivializes an important religious event. If there is anything that Sunday should *not* be for, it should not be for catching up on all of the things that we put off during the rest of our lives. First of all, it's probably impossible to catch up anyway, and second, how on earth can a person celebrate the deep mysteries of life and one's achievements and one's needs and one's closest intimate relationships if all one can think about is catching up?

I would call for a reexamination of the role of Sundays. This reexamination should not be done with an eye towards telling people how they should spend their Sundays, but with an eye towards helping them reflect on how they do spend them and how they would really like to spend them. If we could fault ourselves as a Church for one thing about Sundays, it would be that we have not provided exciting alternatives to the trivializing of Sundays from which the popular culture seems to be suffering. We have not provided a vision for the way in which Sunday is important that would stimulate and motivate people to really use it as a day of reflection and regeneration. In addition, those who are the official gatekeepers of Sundays—the religious professionals—need to see how people do spend their time and what their activity means to them. Reflection on the meanings which people invest in Sundays might well inform our religious institutions as to the best way to assist them in developing their sensibilities and strengthening their awareness of the mythic power this day contains.

The Future of the Assembly

RICHARD P. MCBRIEN

In this presentation on the future of the assembly, our approach is twofold. The first section deals with principles of ecclesiology, and the second offers a method for applying theology to local practice.

I. ECCLESIOLOGY IN PRINCIPLE

1. *To speak about the future of the assembly is to speak about the future of the Church itself.* The "assembly" is no more only a part, or subdivision, of the Church than the parish, or local church, is only a part, or subdivision, of the universal Church. The identification of assembly and Church is at once theological and etymological. In the Septuagint, for example, the word *ekklesia* (used 100 times) means "assembly," whether in the sense of "assembling" or of "those assembled." *Ekklesia* was, first of all, a wholly secular term. Only the addition of the word *kyriou* makes it plain that the *ekklesia* is the people or congregation of God (Deut 23:2ff.; Neh 13:1; Mic 2:5). In the Acts of the Apostles, to take an example from the New

---

RICHARD MCBRIEN is Crowley-O'Brien-Walter Professor of Theology at the University of Notre Dame and chairman of the department of theology. He is a past president of the Catholic Theological Society of America and author of twelve books, including the two-volume work *Catholicism*. He is a priest of the archdiocese of Hartford.

Testament, the Jerusalem *assembly* is spoken of as the *ekklesia*: "And on that day a great persecution arose against the church in Jerusalem" (8:1). In Acts 9:31 the word *ekklesia* is used not merely for the Jerusalem community but for that of all Judea, Galilee, and Samaria: "So the church throughout all Judea and Galilee and Samaria had peace and was built up; and walking in the fear of the Lord and in the comfort of the Holy Spirit it was multiplied." According to K. L. Schmidt's standard article on *ekklesia* in Kittel's *Theological Dictionary of the New Testament*, "Accurately to reproduce the biblical use of the word and concept (*ekklesia*), we ought always to say 'assembly (of God)'."

2. *The Church is at once dynamic and stable; it is the community in process of assembling, and it is the assembled community. How* we assemble and *who is* assembled is at least as important as *how many* are assembled.

3. *The Church, in this case, is either the Church universal or, more immediately, the local community of faith,* summoned by the preached word of God, gathered around the Eucharistic table, and bonded together in the service of one another and of others outside the community. The Church was, in the first instance, a community of local churches, not only churches of particular cities and towns, but even of *house churches.*[1] Only later—in Ephesians, for example—does the idea of the Church universal emerge, linked to Christ as the fullness of creation itself. The Church universal, however, is not simply the sum total of all local churches, any more than we are simply the sum total of our body's individual cells and organs.

4. *The Church is at once Catholic and ecumenical.* The point of reference for most readers is undoubtedly the Catholic assem-

---

1. E.g., Rom 16:3-5: "Greet Prisca and Aquila, my fellow workers in Christ Jesus, who risked their necks for my life, to whom not only I but also all the churches of the Gentiles give thanks; greet also the church in their house." See also 1 Cor 16:19; Col 4:15; Phlm v. 2.

bly (whether in the Roman Catholic sense or the wider sense of the term, embracing Oriental Orthodox, Anglicans, Lutherans, and others). But what is true of the Catholic assembly is essentially true for all others. Differences occur in the way in which the Catholic assembly structures itself for mission: e.g., Petrine ministry and its relation to the college of bishops.

5. *The mission of such a Church or assembly (dynamic/stable; universal/ local; Catholic/ecumenical) is essentially the same as that gathering and mission of those gathered in Jerusalem:* "And they devoted themselves to the apostles' teaching and fellowship, to the breaking of bread and the prayers. And fear came upon every soul; and many wonders and signs were done through the apostles. And all who believed were together and had all things in common; and they sold their possessions and goods and distributed them to all, as any had need. And day by day, attending the temple together and breaking bread in their homes, they partook of food with glad and generous hearts, praising God and having favor with all the people" (Acts 2: 42-47). The mission of the assembly—of *each* assembly— therefore is: (1) *the proclamation of the word of God* ("Jesus is Lord" and "Repent and be baptized . . . in the name of Jesus Christ . . ."); (2) *the celebration of the sacraments*; (3) *the creation and sustaining of a community-life* as a sign, or sacrament, of the Spirit's abiding presence and power and as a foretaste of that perfect community beyond history to which we are called; and (4) *the service of those in need*, whether inside or outside the assembly of God. The assembly, of course, not only proclaims the word of God but is itself judged by it.[2] The assembly not only celebrates the sacraments but is called to *be* itself a sacrament of Christ and of the kingdom of God.[3] The assembly not only

---

2. See Vatican II Dogmatic Constitution on Divine Revelation, no. 10.
3. See Vatican II Dogmatic Constitution on the Church, no. 1.

speaks on behalf of justice and human rights but is itself called to practice justice and to respect the rights of its own members.[4]

6. *Liturgy, therefore, is at the core of the Church's mission, but it is not the whole of that mission.* "The liturgy is the summit toward which the activity of the Church is directed; at the same time it is the fountain from which all her power flows. . . . [But] the sacred liturgy does not exhaust the entire saving activity of the Church."[5]

7. *Local assemblies, or parishes, have differed and will always differ in their missionary activity in accordance with their distinctive self-understandings, or ecclesiologies.* A highly institutional and hierarchical understanding of Church has produced in the past (and present) parishes that were communities in name only. They were (or are) governed unilaterally, and the mission tended to be restricted to a particular form of word and sacrament (the so-called filling-station concept of parish). A highly communitarian (People of God) concept of Church may generate a parish that is acutely conscious of itself as a fellowship, indeed a worshiping fellowship, but perhaps less conscious of its broader responsibilities in the social and political realms. A highly liberationist, or service-oriented, concept of Church can shape a given assembly into an agent of social and political change, but its attention to the word and the sacraments in their broader historical meaning (i.e., over and above their direct applicability to issues of justice, peace, and human rights) may be correspondingly diminished. There is probably least "danger" of the third happening in our situation, however.

4. "Justice in the World," Third International Synod of Bishops, 1971: "While the Church is bound to give witness to justice, it recognizes that anyone who ventures to speak to people about justice must first be just in their eyes."

5. Constitution on the Sacred Liturgy, nos. 10, 9.

8. *Ecclesiology is inevitably expressed in the life and actual practice of given assemblies.* In light of the preceding considerations, therefore, where do our particular assemblies stand? How consistent is their life and practice with the ecclesiological meaning of assembling at the call of God?

II. ECCLESIOLOGY IN PRACTICE

Several weeks ago I completed another semester's course on the Church. As I often do during the final session, I invited the students (a reasonably broad cross section of more than fifty laity, religious, and clergy) to apply the theology we had done together. I asked them to suppose that they had been appointed pastor of a parish or had been hired as a consultant to evaluate a parish, or equivalent Christian community. To what sort of questions would they want answers? By what sort of criteria would they measure the parish? The following is drawn from a checklist we produced together and which I edited for a column and then again for this Conference. I submit that every single item—there are eighteen—has immediate ecclesiological significance.

1. *The quality of Sunday worship.* It is not enough to ask whether worship is central to the life of the parish. Is there a planning process? Is there a broad distribution of ministerial roles? To what extent are men and women alike involved ministerially? What kinds of materials and aids for worship are available? What about space and time for celebration (the environment)? How does the liturgy relate to other activities inside and outside the parish? (E.g., is there a social gathering after Mass? Does the preaching link the Gospel with justice issues?)

2. *The total sacramental life of the parish.* How are the other sacraments celebrated? How central, for example, is the Rite of Christian Initiation of Adults? Is the parish at large involved

in the formation and reception of new members into the community? Indeed, all sacraments are supposed to be community celebrations. In fact, do we create subcommunities for First Communion, First Reconciliation, or Confirmation? Are the only people who are really involved the children and parents or relatives?

3. *Ongoing formation*. What is the quality of the religious education program? Is there sufficient emphasis on adult education? Is there a school? What is its budget? Is the school of high quality? Is it needed? Is it the *normal* educational activity which spills over for the sake of all children? Is there a ministry to youth?

4. *Budget*. What are the financial and human resources? How are they allocated? By what process? What are the sources of funds? Is the budget published?

5. *Organizational structure*. How do things actually work? What kinds of positions are on the organizational chart? How are decisions reached?

6. *Selection of leadership*. How are various ministers selected? What is done to encourage and form leaders from within the parish for service in the wider community? Are there opportunities for women to preside at liturgical services rather than just give a homily? Are the leaders accountable? What provisions are there for the continuing education of the various ministerial leaders?

7. *Life-style of leadership*. Do the ministerial leaders faithfully and credibly reflect the ideals of the parish itself? On the other hand, are ministers treated justly in terms of salary, benefits, and contracts ("Justice in the World")? Are "impressive" religious hired in preference to more qualified lay ministers?

8. *Time management.* What do people on the organizational chart actually do? How long does it take them to do what they do? Some people think the effectiveness of ministry is proportioned to the number of hours and amount of energy expended. But quantity and quality are not the same.

9. *Physical plant.* Are the buildings suitable for their purposes? What do some people mean, for example, when they say that a new church "doesn't even look like a church?"

10. *Social services.* What service does the parish provide for persons and families in crisis, the elderly, the unemployed, ethnic groups, refugees, the divorced, the handicapped, the mentally ill, the sick?

11. *Collegiality.* How does the parish relate to the diocese, the national Church, and the Church universal? (E.g., does the kind of leadership exercised at the diocesan level, or the kind of resources available there, make any significant difference, for good or for ill, within the parish itself?) What sense of responsibility does a wealthy parish have toward the needier parishes of a diocese, or a prosperous diocese toward a needier diocese, or an affluent national Church toward the Third World?

12. *Ecumenism.* What contacts are there with other religious communities, Christian and non-Christian alike? Are there opportunities for joint worship and prayer? If everything is focused on Eucharist alone, there are only limited opportunities for ecumenical prayer. Is there collaboration in the social apostolate?

13. *Relationship with the wider community.* What links does the parish have with social agencies, other churches, city or town government, the diocese, the national Church, the Church universal?

14. *Composition.* Who belongs to the parish? Who are its natural leaders? What are the parishioners' economic status, political views, theological attitudes, and religious values? What is the racial and ethnic makeup of the parish? What are the trends? How much attrition has there been in recent years? What sort of shifts have there been in membership? Who are the alienated? *Why* are they alienated?

15. *Fellowship/Community.* Is there a community here? Or is it a filling station? How does it manifest itself as community? What strains are placed on it? What means are employed to cultivate it?

16. *Communications.* How does the community communicate: leaders to community at large, community at large to leaders, community at large to wider community, etc.? Is it enough simply to announce some need and then give a name and telephone number?

17. *Community's self-description.* What does the parish say about itself in its bulletins, letters, pamphlets, and mission statement?

18. *Ongoing evaluation.* Is there a process for the ongoing evaluation of the parish? Who has input into the process? We tend to be strong in assessing needs and engaging in planning, but weak in seriously evaluating what we have really accomplished.

This may not be a complete checklist, but it would keep any conscientious pastoral leader or consultant busy for a long time. To the extent that this evaluation process is already going on, the future of the assembly is opening up before our eyes. And, to that same extent, it can be a bright and hopeful future indeed.

The Shape of the Future:
A Liturgist's Vision

MARK SEARLE

It takes a certain courage—or a certain foolhardiness—to predict the shape of the future. The future of the Catholic Sunday in America, like so many aspects of life in the years ahead, will be shaped by factors which, even to the skilled futurologist, remain difficult or impossible to anticipate. In years to come, as in the past, the shape of Sunday practice among Christian communities will be the result not only of their religious convictions but also of the social, economic, and cultural factors with which those convictions will have to contend. It may well be, for example, that the trend towards reduced working hours will continue, but that does not guarantee that people will have more free time or that they will devote that free time to religious affairs. Similarly, there are indications, even now, that people are yearning for a return to simpler times and to old-fashioned values,[1] yet it is probable that their picture of the past is at best selec-

1. *The Unchurched American* (Princeton, N.J.: The Princeton Religion Research Center and the Gallup Organization, Inc., 1978) 5-6.

MARK SEARLE is associate director of the Notre Dame Center for Pastoral Liturgy and concurrently associate professor of liturgical studies at the University of Notre Dame. He holds a doctorate in liturgical studies from the theological faculty of Trier, Germany, and is widely known as a lecturer and writer.

tive and idealized; the chances of such nostalgia providing a program for the future are slim indeed. More encouragingly, perhaps, there is also evidence of a deep spiritual hunger among our people; but the same opinion poll that reveals that hunger also reveals a profound lack of confidence in the ability of the institutional churches to respond to that hunger.[2]

On the surface, Sunday in America seems to be in fairly good shape, especially in comparison with the level of religious practice in other Western nations.[3] Yet the unease which fills many pastoral workers and which, in part at least, prompted the choice of this theme for this year's Conference is not without foundation. Sunday church-attendance figures remain high in America, but when one begins to ask what such attendance is understood to mean, problems begin to surface. In the Christian tradition, Sunday, as the day of assembly, is the day when the Church becomes visible and tangible in local congregations. Sunday morning—such is our tradition—is above all the time at which we become what we are called to be: the gathered People of God, the Body of Christ united in the Holy Spirit. Yet the same Gallup survey cited earlier reveals that such an idea is foreign to most Americans.[4] Not surprisingly, perhaps, 88 percent of unchurched Americans claimed that it was possible to be a good Christian without attending church. More significantly, however, 70 percent of church members in this country professed the same belief. In other words, nearly three-quarters of those who claimed to be practicing church members lacked

2. *Ibid.* 8.

3. For a comparison of European and American patterns of religious practice, see Bryan Wilson, *Religion in Secular Society* (London: C. A. Watts & Co., 1966) 86–124. Wilson argues (p. 98) that in America, "though religious practice has increased, the vacuousness of popular religious ideas has also increased: the content and meaning of religious commitment has been acculturated."

4. *The Unchurched American* 41.

any sense of their Christian identity as being essentially a corporate one. Their Christian faith, it would appear, is so distorted by the individualism of the culture that one of the key elements of the Christian vision is either unknown or irrelevant to them.

Thus, despite the apparent strength of the Christian churches in this country, we are in fact confronted with a serious crisis about what it means to be a Christian. Most believers appear to regard religious commitment as a matter of what the U.S. Government likes to call on its official forms "the religion of your choice." Such a view is clearly incompatible with such fundamental Christian themes as those of being called by God, incorporated into the Body Mystical of Jesus Christ, and receiving a new identity in virtue of the one Spirit of holiness which we all share. Sunday in our tradition is the day on which we remember our common identity, but since that sense of a common identity appears to have been eroded by the peculiar religiosity of our culture, it would seem that the Christian Sunday is in serious jeopardy, if it is not dead already.

As I have already suggested, the shape of the future in this matter is not something which can be predicted on the basis of demographic trends. Factors unknown and unforeseen will contribute to that shape—but so will our own convictions and subsequent actions. The question that faces us is whether we shall be content to sit back and see what happens, or whether we shall clarify our perspectives and then work for their realization. First let us clarify our perspectives and then let us consider some options in the light of those perspectives.

I. Perspectives on Sunday

The difficulty about putting Sunday into perspective is that it is tied up with the whole meaning of Christian existence.

As first day of the week, Sunday is a commemorative celebration of what lies at the very heart of the Christian life: God's triumph over sin and death in the exaltation of Jesus. It is thus symbolic of the dawn of a new age: it is the day on which that new age *first* became visible in the resurrection of Jesus and the day on which it *continues* to become visible in the assembly of the baptized, whose congregating is both the fruit of God's redemptive work and the means of its continuation throughout time and space. Thus it is not the day on which, conveniently, individuals and families may simply attend the worship service of their choice; it is rather the day when those summoned by God to work together for his kingdom are called together to renew the covenant they made with him in baptism, when they were plunged into the death of Christ and raised in the Spirit to form a new humanity. But there, precisely, is the rub. Only those with a vivid sense of their own baptismal identity can begin to live out God's project for the world. Put very bluntly: Sunday can be lived and appreciated only by those who have died, for *Sunday is the time of life-after-death*.

Of course, there are various ways of thinking about death, and each colors the way we think about life-before-death and life-after-death. These outlooks, in turn, color the way we think about Sunday.

One obvious way to think about death is to think of it as the termination of life, as an exit from history, as a leaving behind of the things of life. Such a view has been common enough in Christianity, with the result that Christians have often adopted rather ambivalent attitudes about the things of life. What is meant here by "the things of life" is well expressed by John Dunne in his book *Time and Myth*. Dunne borrows the description of Ecclesiastes: "There is a season for everything and a time for every purpose under heaven." Dunne continues:

The things that are named by Koheleth are all the seasonal activities of man: being born and dying, planting and uprooting, killing and healing, tearing down and building up, weeping and laughing, mourning and dancing, scattering and gathering, embracing and holding apart, seeking and giving up, keeping and casting away, rending and sewing, keeping silence and speaking, loving and hating, making war and making peace. Each of them has its time.

And John Dunne comments: "If there is a life in man that can survive death, it is none of these."[5]

Because the life that survives death cannot be identified with these things of life, Christians have tended to see them as alternatives to, or distractions from, the life of the world to come. This has resulted in a concept of perfection which identifies it with the greatest possible detachment from the things of life. This even entered our liturgy, especially through the prayers, where such phrases as *doceas nos terrena despicere et amare celestia* (teach us to turn away from the things of earth and to love those of heaven) seemed repeatedly to set life-before-death in contrast with life-after-death.[6] The impression given is that there is a radical discontinuity between the conditions of historical existence and the life of the world to come, so that people serious about the latter can only be wary of the former. In this kind of asceticism, death is the point of discontinuity, the termination of life, which we await and to which the pious soul looks forward with yearning.

In marked contrast to this view, though still sharing the supposition that death is an event that occurs at the end of life, is the attitude of our own culture. Many people today still cling to private belief in life-after-death, but our culture

5. John S. Dunne, *Time and Myth* (Notre Dame, Ind.: University of Notre Dame Press, 1973) 12.

6. Prayer After Communion, Second Sunday of Advent, *Missale Romanum* (New York: Benziger Brothers, 1962) 4. See Placide Bruylants, "Terrena despicere et amare caelestia," in *Miscellanea Liturgica in onore de S.E. il Card. Giacomo Lercaro*, II (Rom: Desclée, 1967) 195–206.

as such has nothing to say about it. It is rather characterized
by its forgetfulness of death. It can afford to be forgetful
of death because it is dominated not by people, who must
die, but by collective processes that can go on indefinitely.
Collective life transcends the personal cycle of birth and
death, survives the death of the individual. It is something
that exists as more than the sum of the lives of the individuals
that make up the collective process. It has a life of its own;
we are constantly exhorted to throw ourselves into it and to
get the most out of it. We enter it, are caught up in it, leave
it—and it goes on without us.

But this collective life consists precisely of the things
for which there is a season and the purposes for which there
is a time. It is an endless succession of acquiring, using, and
disposing: of producing goods and services to create wealth
which we can then turn back into the system through our
use and consumption. It is a life which makes every goal the
means to attaining some further goal: production is for the
sake of consumption which is for the sake of production;
work is undertaken to pay for the leisure which refreshes
us for work.

Life in our society tends to become defined in terms of—
and in the service of—this process. Throwing ourselves into
this "life" means ceasing to live an independent, personal
existence in order to become part of the collective process.
It means living an existence which is not only dominated
by collective, impersonal processes but also oriented towards
objects of exchange. But these impersonal forces of production and the impersonal statistics of consumption have
the effect of rendering us, in our turn, impersonal units of
productivity and consumption. Our value is derived from our
role as producers and consumers. As this happens, we ourselves become subject to the very same criteria of useful-
ness and expendability to which we subject other things
and other people. It used to be, for example, that age and

experience counted for something, but now what counts is to be "up to date." We talk of people being "recycled" and the best we can find to say about the elderly is that they still manage to keep up, that they continue to be "productive."

Thus the very cycle which defies death by surviving us is also the treadmill of our servitude. We become subservient to the project of our society: the achievement of ever vaster processes of production and consumption. In so doing, we learn to identify ourselves as producers and consumers, losing any sense of our own inner identity. A society which can keep rolling along, unperturbed by death, is a society which is necessarily anonymous: it identifies people by their role, not by their name. The name dies, the role goes on. Conversely, it is confrontation with death which makes us aware of our own personal uniqueness. If "soul" is the name we give to the principle of relating to our own identity and destiny, then our society, in its very call to throw ourselves into this collective life, is soul-destroying. Deprived of identity, deprived of autonomy, we find ourselves being born and dying, planting and uprooting, dancing and mourning anonymously, as part of the faceless collectivity, moving to the rhythm of the clock, the humming of the machines, the opening of the supermarkets. Under the illusion of suiting our own purposes, we become in fact admirably suited to the purposes of the system, mere workers and consumers who fade in and out of the remorseless socio-economic process. In such a context, it is clear that the three-day weekend has nothing to do with the Christian Sunday: it is simply the phase when the time of production yields to the time of consumption. "If there is a life in man that can survive death, it is none of these."

But there is another view of death which sees it not as the termination of life, but as an event within life itself. The paradox of Christianity is that we are a people who have faced death and survived it. "You have been taught that when

we were baptized in Christ Jesus, we were baptized in his
death . . . we went into the tomb with him and joined him in
death" (Rom 6:3-4). In the letter to the Colossians (2:20-21),
we are asked: "If you have really died with Christ to the
principles of this world, why do you still let rules dictate you,
as if you were still living in the world?" We have seen what
it means to live in the world and to be subject to its principles,
subject to the impersonal imperatives of production and
consumption, of obsolescence and recycling. But what would
it mean to live with death behind us? What would it do to us
to see death as something we had already lived through, so
that we were already living life-after-death, the life of the
world to come?

Anyone who has had a close encounter with death, or—
what amounts to the same thing—the experience of a crisis
which, at least temporarily, suspends the customary patterns
of life, will know the overwhelming power of such an experience to do two things. First, it has the power to engage
us inescapably as persons: it is *I* who am undergoing this, and
I am inescapably confronted with who I am, perhaps for the
first time. Second, such an experience has the effect of rendering all our other engagements relatively unimportant:
what seemed to matter ceases to matter, previous anxieties
now seem foolish, attitudes and ambitions now appear ab-
surd. On the other hand, so many things which had gone
unnoticed, so many people hitherto taken for granted, now
seem newly dear and precious, as if we were seeing them
and appreciating them for the first time. Such an experience
has the effect of propelling us, as it were, out of the gravita-
tional pull of the world's atmosphere to a point where we
can look upon life precisely as gift, seeing it and all that enters
into it, with greater clarity and simplicity.

To come back from the dead, then, would be to see people
and things not as objects to be used for our own purposes,
but as they are in themselves. It would be to know the truth

of things as they are and to cherish them as such. Instead of producing in order to consume and consuming in order to produce, it would be to follow the advice of the *Bhagavadgita*, "Act without seeking the fruits of action."[7] In other words, when you build a house, let it be building a house, not just building in order to sell. When you serve a client, let it be for the sake of the client, not just for the wage. When you cook, let it be for the sake of the food, not just for the eating. When you eat, let it be with grateful appreciation, not just ingesting to provide energy for something else. When you plant, let it be with respect for the seed and the soil, not for the profit. When you dance, let it be for the sake of the dance, not for display. When you laugh or mourn, let the tears and the laughter be prompted not by the success or failure of your own purposes, but by the happiness or sorrow of another. In a word, whereas those who live-before-death live in a world of using and being used, those who live already the life of the world-to-come relate personally to the things of life and to the people they encounter.

Such, too, is the effect of sharing in the death of Christ. It is, above all, liberation from the tyranny of collective principles, release from the treadmill of doing and having. It opens our eyes to see that it is who we are, not what we possess or produce, that is capable of surviving death. As John Dunne says, "The things that come to an end in death are all the things that have their proper time and season in life. Spirit is not one of these, but is rather man's relationship to each and all of them."[8] Baptismal death is entry into the life of the Spirit, the life of being free and of setting free. To us who have died, it is given to transform the relationships that constitute human existence, to renew the face of the earth.

7. See *The Song of God: Bhagavad-Gita,* trans. Swami Prabharananda and Christopher Isherwood, (New York: New American Library) 40, 52, and *passim.*

8. Dunne, *Time and Myth* 13.

For this reason, the Christian Sunday differs radically from the three-day weekend and even from the Jewish sabbath. The weekend marks the switch from earning to spending. The sabbath is a day of rest from labor in anticipation of the rest of God which preceded creation and will follow history.[9] Sunday represents an altogether more radical idea: that the age to come is already here and that it lasts not from sunset on Friday to sundown on Saturday, or from Friday evening to Monday morning, but from the dawn of Christ's resurrection on the first day of the week unto ages of ages. Sunday is the "Eighth Day" because it celebrates the incursion of life-after-death into the lives and history of the human race, shattering the treadmill of the seven-day week—even of the four-day week—and bringing a new way of relating to the things of life.

Sunday also differs from the sabbath in that it is a day of assembly. It is not, like the sabbath, a day that is holy in itself, but a day upon which Christians—those who have survived death—emerge from the camouflage of lives lived quietly in an unbelieving world—the world of the undead—and are seen, or at least see themselves, for what they are: the firstfruits of the age to come, the beginning of a new humanity freed from servitude to anonymous, impersonal, death-defying processes to serve the living God.

Sunday is thus the day when the Christian community, in assembling, renews its baptismal identity, proclaiming not only the death of the Lord but its own death in the thanksgiving sacrifice of the Eucharist. Finally, it has been a day when, more than any other but not to the exclusion of any other, Christians have experimented with the radical implications of living life-beyond-death in this world, trying to relate to the things of life as people who already live the life of the world-to-come.

9. Abraham Heschel, *The Sabbath* (New York: Farrar, Strauss & Giroux, 1951).

II. Options For Sunday

If the American Catholic community is ever to recover a sense of the place of Sunday in its life, it will have to be faithful to these perspectives and to the tradition from which it draws its identity. That tradition provides us with three structural elements which shape both Sunday observance and the lives of those who have passed from death to life. These three structural elements are assembly, word, and paschal sacraments.

1. The Assembly

As we have already remarked, the identity of the Church and of the individual Christian is tied to the weekly assembly. Scripturally, theologically, and liturgically, there can be no Christians without Church, no Church without assembly. Centuries of cultural and spiritual individualism have largely obscured this baptismal motif, with the result that we have little sense of ourselves as a people animated by a single life, the life of the Spirit of Christ. The precept to attend Sunday Mass under pain of mortal sin is a true, if distorted, expression of what was once expressed more positively in the exhortation not to dismember the Body of Christ by staying away from the assembly.[10]

On the other hand, if assembling is indispensable to being Church, it is also insufficient. Assembly presupposes the common life out of which it arises, a common life which makes us members of one another in Christ even when we

---

10. *The Didascalia of the Apostles*, ch. 13: "When you are teaching, command and exhort the people to be faithful to the assembly of the Church. Let them not fail to attend, but let them gather faithfully together. Let no one deprive the Church by staying away; if they do, they deprive the Body of Christ of one of its members! . . . Do not, then, make light of your own selves, do not deprive our Saviour of his members, do not rend, do not scatter his Body!" (English translation by Matthew J. O'Connell in Lucien Deiss, *Springtime of the Liturgy* (Collegeville: The Liturgical Press, 1979) 176–77.

are not assembled together. In the past, the shape of that common life has varied considerably. In the early Church, the community consisted of a social network within a heterogeneous society. In the era of Christendom, the Church was happy to capitalize upon existing forms of natural community in towns, villages, and estates. For a long time in this country, immigrants could find a home away from home in the ethnic communities clustered around their own national churches; but with the assimilation of immigré Catholics into the wider American society, the sociological basis of Catholic community and its Sunday assembly has become problematic. It seems probable that in the years ahead the Catholic Church is going to have to come to terms with its post-immigrant status. We shall have to reassess our attachment to social patterns which have either ceased to exist or have been seriously eroded and be open to the discovery of new forms of association and community living. Indeed, the fostering of new forms of community could well be part of our mission to the larger society.

However, if the shape of Christian community has taken so many different forms in the past, it is clear that what is important for the future is not so much what specific forms might develop as what sense of identity might inspire them. According to sociologist Jacqueline Scherer, the essentials for any sense of community are "a collective perspective, agreed-upon definitions, and some agreement about values."[11] It is here that the importance of the Sunday assembly becomes apparent. While the liturgical assembly cannot provide a sense of community itself, it nevertheless rehearses the Christian account of the meaning of existence and invites the faithful to reaffirm their commitment to the common perspectives, definitions, and values which

11. Jacqueline Scherer, *Contemporary Community* (London: Tavistock Publications, 1972) 122.

bond and identify people as members of the Christian community.[12] Given the problems of isolation and anonymity in today's society, it is hardly surprising that parishes should be putting so much emphasis on building community, but the warning of Andrew Greeley should be heeded: "Community can't be rushed or sought directly and self-consciously. . . . Men must have something to do together before they can become a community and those who pursue community as an end in itself will be as disappointed as those who pursue happiness as an end in itself."[13]

There are many kinds of human community. Among them there is Christian community, a community with its own specific identity. This identity, we have suggested, derives from the fact that all its members have passed through death and are called to live, on this earth, the life of the world-to-come. The importance of the Sunday assembly is not that it can, of itself, create community, but that it continually reminds us of who we are and invites us to reaffirm our commitment. A sense of community is one of those things which will be given those who seek first the kingdom of God. The Church is not something that exists for its own sake: it is a by-product of life in the kingdom of God. Liturgical celebration, then, should not be guided by the quest for community but should be allowed simply to proclaim the perspectives, definitions, and values of gospel life-after-death. In this way it will continually deepen, purify, and correct our common life in the Spirit.

It may well happen that the growing phenomenon of neighborhood groups and service groups in parishes will offer more and more Catholics the opportunity to identify

12. François Houtart, "Sociologie de la paroisse comme assemblée eucharistique," *Paroisse et Liturgie* 45, no. 6 (1963) 558–572. See also the author's "Aspects sociologiques du role de la liturgie dans la vie ecclésiale: communication, socialization, appartenance," *La Maison-Dieu* 91 (1967) 105–128.

13. Quoted in J. Scherer, *Contemporary Community* 120.

with other Catholics and to find there the support and stimulus they need. If that does happen, one could foresee that the practice of multiplying Masses throughout the weekend could begin to be called into question as people begin to recognize the minimalism that is implicit in the practice. New forms of association are likely to breed new liturgical expectations. The danger is, perhaps, that such small groups might become introverted and somewhat cut off from the larger community and would want to find all their needs, including their liturgical and sacramental needs, met in the narrow circle of their own group. Ideally, the Sunday assembly of the faithful and the meetings of smaller groups would have the effect of calling each other to greater realization of what it means to be a people who already live the life of the world-to-come. This realization, celebrated in parish liturgy, would then in turn give rise to the broader concerns which have traditionally been associated with the community's celebration of the Sunday Eucharist: the care of the sick and needy, visiting the imprisoned, caring for the marginal and neglected.[14] In modern terms, these traditional Sunday observances would translate, perhaps, into such preoccupations as concern with neighborhood issues, environmental issues, and global political issues. It is an illusion to think that any Christian community ever has been or ever will be one-hundred percent committed to living out its Christian identity. The role of liturgy, consequently, is never just to celebrate what we already are, but to offer a critical image of what we are called to be. For that reason, it must never be manipulated into being an affirmation of any given form of community or celebration of togetherness. It continually calls us beyond the sociological realities of community— whether they be ethnic, geographical, or even claim to be

14. Adalbert Hamman, *The Grace to Act Now: Liturgy and the Apostolate in the Light of the Early Christian Communities* (Chicago: Franciscan Herald Press, 1966).

"countercultural"—to constant discovery of the oneness of all humanity in Christ, transcending all identifying boundaries.[15]

2. Hearing the Word

A major constituent of postconciliar liturgical reform was the Council's concern for a more adequate proclamation of the word of God. This concern led to the drawing up of a new lectionary and to new insistence on the importance of the liturgical homily. The pastoral task of the future, however, will have to focus on the other end of the communications process: that of *hearing* the word of God. Serious attention to the conditions for a more effective hearing of the word may well be a significant factor in determining the shape of the Sunday assembly in the future.

One significant factor in communications breakdown, of course, is always a lack of attention or readiness to hear on the part of the addressee. This is particularly important where the word of God is concerned, for the readiness to hear implies a willingness to be converted, to have one's life transformed. Discussion of what is required in terms of personal preparedness to hear the word would take us too far afield, but we might remark in passing that it certainly requires some degree of freedom from the turmoil and tur-

15. Sociologist David Martin writes: "From the unity of God springs the unity of the people of God, the unity of the human race, the unity of belief, the unity of human speech. Implicit in unity is the concept of something absolutely inclusive, and that in turn implies exclusion. Unity creates duality and encounters diversity. In the Jewish case, of course, the impulse to unity is held in check by the fact that the truth is located on a biological basis, the peoplehood of Israel. This lowers the tension with diversity, and all but destroys any impulse to bring everybody into the one fold. The capsule of the peculiar people does not expand or take off: it stays as an irreducible peculiarity, co-existing with other peoples." *The Breaking of the Image: A Sociology of Christian Theory and Practice* (Oxford: Basil Blackwell, 1980) 12. Perhaps something similar has happened in American Catholicism, given the close association of ethnic identity and religious belonging.

bulence of life and that the tradition of Sunday rest might
have something important to offer by way of disciplining
us to hear the word of God. Here we shall be content to make
some simple remarks about the context and structure within
which the word of God is proclaimed.

British sociologist Bryan Wilson argues that the major
difference between the kind of communication which characterizes present-day society and that which characterized
previous societies has less to do with the shift from the written to the spoken word than with the shift from the personal
spoken word to the impersonal spoken word.[16] It used to
be that knowledge was communicated by one person to
another and concerned a shared and more or less familiar
world, but now the acquisition, storage, retrieval, and publication of information has become a vast process dealing
with masses of impersonal items of knowledge. "Such a
change at once affects the extent of what is known; more
people share a certain body of fact, but the source of that
fact is no longer located in the community structure as—
for most people—it was in the past."[17] The result is that we
no longer regard information as linking us to one another
and to a common world: it is just a vast amassing of facts.
In such a context, the reading of Scripture and the preaching of Christian doctrine and morals tend likewise to be seen
as just another body of impersonal facts not related to, still
less derived from, the experience of the local Christian community. Yet, as Wilson goes on to point out, "the model of
relationships, the moral prescriptions and the assumptions
about human life embraced in traditional religion are heavily
dependent upon personal experience of community struc-

16. Bryan Wilson, "Unbelief as an Object of Research," *The Culture of
Unbelief*, ed. R. Caporale and A. Gremelli (Berkeley and London: University
of California Press, 1971) 262-63.

17. *Ibid.* 263.

ture and are adapted to it."[18] In other words, the word of God is not the communication of a body of doctrine and morals so much as a personal invitation to union with God and with one another.

Yet we proclaim this personal word in a way which has the inevitable effect of rendering it impersonal. The practice of reading snippets of the Old and New Testaments before a congregation of several hundred people and then commenting upon them in a homily addressed to no one in particular can only confirm the misapprehension that the word of God is a body of remote and esoteric knowledge. This practice assumes, for one thing, that everyone in the congregation is at the same level in their faith-journey, whereas in reality the average congregation comprises not only age-groups from the infant to the elderly, but some of us who are wrestling with our faith and others of us who never think twice about it; some who are closely involved in parish life and others who are quite peripheral and anonymous; some who are present out of sheer spiritual desperation and others who are only desperate to get out and get on to other things. In such conditions, it can only be by accident that anyone present actually hears the word of God. The parable of the sower (Mark 4:1-9) who sowed his seed so indiscriminately upon field and footpath alike represents an *a posteriori* recognition of the generosity of God, not an *a priori* principle about proclaiming the word in a way which makes its hearing a matter of indifference. If the word of God had been proclaimed in apostolic times as it is today, the Church would never have got off the ground!

In view of this, it would seem important to give serious consideration to Joseph Gelineau's suggestion to provide a variety of forums for the proclamation of the word on Sundays, where the needs of different groups of people

18. *Ibid.*

could be met.[19] The Annual Conference of the Notre Dame Center for Pastoral Liturgy remains a single conference, even though people go off to attend different sessions simultaneously. Perhaps the Sunday assembly could be organized along similar lines, so that after an informal gathering of all the people, parishioners could then break up into different groups according to their needs. Provision could be made, as is already frequently the case, for children to play, learn, and celebrate together, while adults could meet with other adults for a common confrontation with the word of God presented in a way best suited to their needs. The same Scripture readings, though not necessarily all three, could serve as a common point of departure; but while one group focused on basic evangelization, another could move to shared prayer, another to investigating personal spirituality, another to looking at the mission of the local community, and so on. Such groups would not exclude there being a main assembly as well, in which the word could be celebrated more solemnly and ritually through reading, singing, dancing, and preaching. The whole community could then reassemble for a summary of the word of the day, for common prayer, and for the celebration of Eucharist. Perhaps lunch would follow, in the style of a parish picnic, to be followed in the afternoon by opportunity for relaxation or for further study or for planning and coordinating community projects. The afternoon could conclude with the festive celebration of vespers before all disperse to their homes to enjoy the rest of the day in the more intimate circle of family and friends.

Such a scenario, or something like it, would go a long way towards providing the kind of interaction which would enable the word to be more effectively heard and acted upon. It would thereby foster a real sense of common values and

19. Joseph Gelineau, "Église—Assemblées—Dimanche. Reflexions et perspectives pastorales," *La Maison-Dieu* 124 (1975) 85–109. See his book *The Liturgy Today and Tomorrow* (Paramus, N.J.: Paulist Press, 1978) 36ff.

provide a more realistic context for the celebration of baptism and Eucharist.

3. The Paschal Sacraments

The response to the Gospel of death and resurrection is the celebration of the sacraments of our participation in that death and resurrection: baptism and Eucharist. The earliest description we have of how Christians celebrated Sunday comes from the pen of Justin Martyr, writing at Rome *ca.* 160.[20] His description of the liturgy of word and Eucharist follows closely upon his description of baptism and Eucharist, and this in such a way as to suggest that the assembly for Sunday Eucharist is above all the occasion for renewing the sense of thanksgiving and commitment proper to those who, in baptism, have experienced God's regenerating power. The baptismal commitment, which he speaks of as "our dedication to God after being created anew through Jesus Christ," takes the form of a shared way of life, marked by a common set of beliefs about the world; a common commitment to a radically new way of life; a common dedication to mutual support, material as well as spiritual; a sense of commitment, too, to the larger world; and a deep sense of thankfulness to God for the new life and vision he has given the baptized.

From Justin's description we see the common prayer of the faithful and the blessing and partaking of the Eucharist gifts contextualized in two complementary dimensions, one personal, the other communitarian. At the personal level, the Eucharist is meaningful, and thus accessible, only to the baptized: i.e., to those who have been "created anew through Jesus Christ." The communal dimension is precisely the common experience of this rebirth and the revolutionary life-style to which it gives rise among the baptized. The

20. *I Apology*, chs. 61—67.

unity of the Church, sacramentalized in the Eucharist—
in which we proclaim the death of the Lord and our own
death until he comes—consists of our common experience
of dying in the midst of life: our common experience of ceasing to be born and to die, to dance and to mourn, to build up
and to pull down, in order to relate to birth and death, to
dancing and mourning, to building and demolishing, as people
who know that life does not consist just of doing these things
but of relating to them as people who know that such things
of life are transformed by the Spirit in which they are done.

In focusing our Eucharistic faith so much as we have on
the transformation of the elements of bread and wine and
on the encounter with Christ in the elements, we have blinded
ourselves to its fuller meaning. The Eucharist is not just a
momentary encounter with the world-to-come, as something breaking in from outside. It is rather the revelation
of a life and presence which already stirs, like a deep, hidden
current, in the life of the world:[21] the life of the risen Christ,
the life of the world-to-come, accessible to us now only
through death in the midst of life. Thus the Eucharist is a
renewed encounter with our own death, first undergone in
baptism, a new detachment from the things that must pass
in order to recover them from the vantage point of a life that
has been touched and transformed by death.

If this is the meaning of Eucharist, however, and if Christianity is not just the memory of what God once did for Jesus,
but the experience of what he continues to do for us and in
us—at the cost of our lives—then it cannot be taken lightly
and multiplied upon demand. Attention to the problem of
enabling the faithful to hear and respond to the word will
eventually begin to affect the way the Eucharist is celebrated.
On the one hand, there should be a growing understanding

21. See Karl Rahner, "Considerations on the Active Role of the Lay
Person in the Sacramental Event," *Theological Investigations*, trans. David
Bourke (New York: Seabury Press, 1976) 14:161–84.

of the sacrificial character of the Eucharist as renewal of the covenant and a rediscovery of the meaning of Eucharist as the sacrament of our organic unity in the life of the Spirit. On the other hand, the recognition that not everyone in the community is at the same stage of growth in the new life should also make it possible for those who are not yet ready for baptism—or for those who, though baptized in infancy, now feel uncertain of their commitment or troubled in their faith—to withdraw from participation in the celebration of the Eucharist in favor of some alternative form of celebration better suited to their condition. The wisdom of the Church has always allowed this, sometimes insisted upon it. Not only were the catechumens ordered to leave as the Eucharist began, but penitents—those who, for reasons of faith or morals, were no longer fully at home in the community of faith—were advised to abstain from the Eucharist, either by withdrawing with the catechumens or by not actually partaking of the Eucharistic gifts.[22] In our present situation, there is no way of acknowledging people's very different situations. It is simply assumed for all public purposes that everyone in the congregation on a Sunday morning is in the same relationship to the Church as everyone else. It would seem more honest, as well as pastorally advantageous, if we were to recognize the very real differences in the community and to help relieve people of the collective pressure which makes it virtually impossible for them to speak openly about real crises of faith or real difficulties with the Christian life-style.

There is room, too, for greater formality and solemnity in the celebration of the Eucharist than has become fashionable in recent years. A more profound understanding of the mystery of the word will perhaps make us more sensitive

---

22. See texts in Paul F. Palmer, *Sacrament and Forgiveness.* Sources of Christian Theology, vol. 2 (Westminster, Md.: Newman Press, 1960).

to the mystery of the Eucharist. Instead of presuming that we know what the rite is about and then altering it to taste, a return to ritual and to reverence will express and foster a more humble and more receptive attitude to the rites themselves and to the mystery they contain.

III. FURTHER DIMENSIONS OF SUNDAY

If one compares Sunday as Catholics celebrate it today with the way it was celebrated even a generation ago, it is clear that one aspect of Sunday has to all intents and purposes disappeared: Sunday rest.

The fact that the first day of the week was a working day like any other for the first centuries of Christianity and the fact that the introduction of the work-free Sunday was not originally a Church-inspired initiative has led some people to think of Sunday rest as an insignificant part of our tradition. This judgment is probably colored by the fact that it would be virtually impossible for Church authorities to enforce it in today's circumstances anyway. Given the casuistry which attended the whole question in modern times, perhaps it is as well that the matter has been allowed to drop for a while. It is clear, for example, that the old categories of servile works and liberal arts have long since ceased to make sense in terms of modern patterns of activity,[23] where the distinction between the labors of servants and the genteel occupations of the leisured classes have completely broken down. The passing of such social distinctions is hardly to be lamented, but the whole question of Sunday rest does need reexamination.

As we saw earlier, the reason why the sabbath was eventually abandoned was not that God had chosen a different day of the week to set apart for himself, but that in Jesus the

23. Hannah Arendt, *The Human Condition* (Chicago: University of Chicago Press, 1958) 90ff., 126ff.

very age which the sabbath anticipated has already arrived. Now God was claiming, as it were, all seven days of the week! No longer would we have one day a week on which to look forward to the joys of the world-to-come; instead, we who have been raised from the dead with Christ are to live our whole existence as citizens of the world-to-come. For us, then, the issue is not simply one of helping people rediscover the meaning of leisure; although that, too, needs to be done for, as has often been remarked, modern people have at last achieved a measure of freedom from toil only to find they have forgotten how to do anything but work.[24]

The issue is actually wider than the question of leisure: it includes our understanding of and approach to work as well. The issue, simply put, is whether we have anything to say to one another and to the world about what it means to be a people who have already passed through death. In a world where everyone builds up and pulls down, seeks and gives away, rends and sews, makes peace and makes war without regard to the day of the week or to how these things are done, do we have anything to say about how such activities might be transformed into personal and communal actions by doing them differently?

What is at stake, then, is not so much the character of the so-called Christian Sunday, but the secret of Christian living itself. This, in turn, depends upon the quality of our common life in the Body of Christ, upon the degree to which the two-edged sword of God's word is allowed to encompass our death, and upon the kind of power the Eucharist is permitted to have among us as a celebration of the life-to-come. In short, the quality of our Christian lives, of which Sunday was once a symbol, depends upon the quality of our Sunday assemblies. But it is also clear that the Sunday assembly will

24. *Ibid.* 320-25. See also Josef Pieper, *In Tune With the World* (Chicago: Franciscan Herald Press, 1973).

never be able to fill the role it was meant to fill in our lives unless we give more time to it. The Gospel is the Good News of our liberation. The Sunday assembly is meant to be the assembly of a liberated people, in which we both acknowledge and claim that freedom from the hand of God who raises us from the dead. But how can we possibly celebrate that freedom if we remain complacent about the pressures under which we live, especially the pressure of time? Mass may not last more than an hour, we are told; people do not have the time. Masses have to be multiplied and held at all sorts of hours to fit into people's schedules. Is that freedom? Did Christ come to liberate us or to feed us through our prison bars?

Hence the importance of Sunday as a work-free day. If we do not claim our freedom on that day, where shall we claim it? If on this day we do not adamantly refuse to live as slaves of necessity, prisoners of society's collective attitudes, victims of social pressure and rampant consumerism, when shall we ever know what it is like to enjoy the freedom of those who have passed through death?

This brings us, finally, to the question of the Sunday obligation. In a very profound sense, "Sunday obligation" is a contradiction in terms—unless it is to be understood in the sense of "much obliged." Sunday is for Christians a symbol and a sacrament of the freedom of the age-to-come, of the future already brought into the present by the resurrection of Jesus and the outpouring of his Spirit. It would probably be better not to attend the Sunday assembly at all than merely to attend out of fear of punishment or pressure to conform.[25] The Sunday Mass obligation is unhelpful if it is perceived as a burden, but its legal formulation is merely the negative aspect of what was once expressed more

25. For some sensible guidelines on Sunday rest, see Christopher Kiesling, *The Future of the Christian Sunday* (New York: Sheed & Ward, 1970) 125–140.

positively: you have been called by God to share his Spirit in the Body of Christ—do not dismember his Body by your absence.

The accent should, in the future, be on the call to freedom, and the kind of thing we do in the Sunday assembly should be such as to confirm us in our freedom. Unfortunately, for most of us human beings, freedom is a heavy burden, and the Church has constantly suffered the temptation to compromise her mission by relieving the faithful of that burden. It is easier to obey than to accept the responsibilities of freedom; it is easier to demand obedience than it is to motivate. Yet that is the difference between this age and the age-to-come. In the long term, the future of Sunday, like the future of Christianity itself, will depend upon our readiness to claim our own freedom (which means, also, to be held accountable) and our ability to extend that freedom to others. The abolition of the Sunday Mass obligation would do little good at this point: it would merely be seen as a change of rules and would thereby contribute further to the terrible trivialization of Christian existence from which we all suffer. More important—and more urgent— is the development of an overall community vision concerning the new life and the new freedom which, through the loving-kindness of our God, has been granted to those who have died with Christ in baptism and been raised to life in the Spirit for the renewal of the face of the earth.

Sunday Rest: A Contemplative Approach to Worship

BENEDICTA BOLAND, O.S.B.

It has become a commonplace in recent years to speak of Sunday as the day of resurrection. Insofar as this serves to correct an understanding of the phrase "the Lord's Day" which identified it in almost sabbatarian terms as the day that belongs to God, speaking of Sunday as the day of resurrection is very helpful. Yet it does not go quite far enough toward suggesting what it was that led the first Christian community to establish the day after the sabbath as the day for assembling and for celebrating the Eucharist in memory of Jesus. The truth of the matter is that Sunday became the day of the Son, the day of the Lord Jesus, not because he was remembered as being raised triumphantly from death on that day, but because it was on that day, when the disciples were together, that they encountered him risen from the dead. The original message of the Church was, "We have seen the Lord!"

The first day of the week was thus the first day of a new age, the age of salvation, the age of God gathering in the

BENEDICTA BOLAND completed her liturgical studies at the Catholic University of America. She is a member of the Benedictine community of Red Plains Priory in Oklahoma City, Oklahoma, and serves as administrator of the Office of Liturgy of the Diocese of Tulsa and executive secretary of the diocesan liturgy commission.

scattered children of his, the age in which the stranglehold of sin and death could now be seen to have been broken: "We have seen the Lord!" It is an alpha and omega day. As alpha, it is a new beginning, the first letter of a new history that God is writing. As omega, it is both the last word of all that has been written hitherto and anticipation of the final triumph of God at the end of all human history. It is thus tied up closely with the person and mission of Jesus, the faithful remnant of the old Israel and the firstborn of the new People of God. It is a day for realizing his resurrection and experiencing the newness of time in these last ages.

Before moving into the main part of this paper, it might be as well simply to recall the main features of the Christian Sunday—the day when the faithful encounter the risen one. This characteristic of the first day of the week as day of encounter is particularly clear from Luke's account of the disciples on the road to Emmaus (24:13-35). Here the memory of God's saving acts in the past sheds light on the meaning of recent events, and the disciples, whose hearts they later realized had been "burning within them," finally recognized the presence of the risen Lord in their midst as they shared the breaking of bread. There are other places in Acts which associate the first day of the week with hearing the word of God and celebrating the breaking of bread (e.g., 20:7-12), so this seems to indicate a recurrent practice.

However, other New Testament hints about the nature of this day should prevent us from assuming too quickly that their "Lord's Day" was the same as ours merely because we read the Scriptures and perform the Eucharistic ritual. For example, it is in the context of a Sunday assembly that Paul suggests to the Corinthians a fairly radical program of mutual support among the faithful: "On the first day of each week everyone should put aside whatever he has been able to save . . ." (1 Cor 16:2f.). Paul claims to have given the same instructions to the communities in Galatia, so he clearly sees the sharing of wealth for the benefit of the poor and the distressed to be an integral part of the act of assembling to meet the Lord. Perhaps another characteristic of the early Christian Sunday is alluded to in Revelation 1:10, where it is explicitly noted that it was on the Lord's day that the seer was caught up in ecstasy while exiled on Patmos and was commanded to write to the seven churches and demand of them more openness to the word of God, a listening ear, and an attentive spirit.

One characteristic of Sunday as we have inherited it is not to be found in the practice of the primitive Church: the practice of Sunday rest, modeled on the Jewish observance of the sabbath as a day of rest. Indeed, the Gospels carry traces of disputes about the nature and importance of the sabbath, not only in the post-Easter community but in the ministry of Jesus himself. Whether or not Jesus abolished the sabbath obligation, as some early Christians claimed, or whether he simply brought new insight into its true character by proclaiming it a day of healing and redemption, it is certain that early Christians did not think of the Sunday assembly as replacing the sabbath. For many of them, the sabbath had been fulfilled, not in the observance of Sunday but in the new era of history opened up by the resurrection of Jesus. If the sabbath celebrated both creation and the redemption of Israel, then the new age inaugurated by Jesus' victory over sin and death was itself a new creation and a new experience of redemption.

The early sources, then, point to a Sunday observance marked by assembly, hearing the word, breaking the Eucharistic bread, and mutual charity. So the early second-century *Didache*:

> Come together on the Lord's day
> break bread and give thanks
> having first confessed your sins
> so that your sacrifice may be pure.

Anyone who has a quarrel with his fellow
should not gather with you
until he has been reconciled
lest your sacrifice be profaned.[1]

The first full description of a Sunday Eucharist is given us by Justin Martyr (*ca.* 160 A.D.). In his first Apology, he not only describes the gathering of people from town and country "on the day named after the sun," the reading of the "memoirs of the apostles," and the breaking of bread, but he speaks of preaching which helps ensure that the word is heard, and of the contributions collected by the president of the community from the wealthy for distribution to "orphans and widows, those who are in want because of sickness or some other reason, those in prison, and visiting strangers."[2] Finally, in the *Apostolic Tradition* of Hippolytus, probably originating in Rome in the early third century, we find that Sunday is an important day for arranging the community's own affairs: "He is to be ordained bishop who has been chosen by the whole people and who is of blameless life. When he has been nominated and accepted by all, let the people assemble on the Lord's day with the presbyters and the bishops who are at hand."[3] The account goes on to direct how the ordination is to take place and how it is to be followed by a celebration of the Eucharist.

These vestiges of the practice of the early centuries of Christianity are enough to give us some feel for the different kinds of experience associated by early Christians with Sunday. It was only in the fourth century, in 321, that the Emperor Constantine, for motives not altogether clear, decreed that Sunday was to be observed every week as a day free

1. *Early Christian Fathers*, ed. Cyril C. Richardson (New York: Macmillan Publishing Co., Inc., 1970) 178.

2. Josef A. Jungmann, S.J., *The Early Liturgy*, trans. Francis A. Brunner (Notre Dame, Ind.: University of Notre Dame Press, 1959) 23.

3. Lucien Deiss, C.S.Sp., *Springtime of the Liturgy*, trans. Matthew J. O'Connell (Collegeville, Minn.: The Liturgical Press, 1979) 127.

from work, with an exception made for those daily chores that farmers had to perform. Thereafter, Christians increasingly tended to interpret Sunday in terms of the fourth commandment of the Decalogue: "Thou shalt keep holy the sabbath day." Not only did they interpret Sunday as a day of rest from labor, but they tended to translate such interpretation into practice, applying the prohibitions of the Jewish sabbath to the activities of Christians on Sunday. It was particularly in the sixth-century councils of Agde (506), Orleans (538), and Macon (585) that the twofold obligation of attendance at Mass and abstinence from servile works came to be imposed. By the thirteenth century, failure to observe the Sunday obligation of rest and worship was regarded by the canonists as gravely sinful.[4] And so it remained until Vatican II.

The purpose of the Council Fathers at Vatican II was not so much to reaffirm inherited legislation about the Sunday obligation as to help Christians come to a deeper appreciation of the original meaning of Sunday:

> By a tradition handed down from the apostles, which took its origin from the very day of Christ's resurrection, the Church celebrates the paschal mystery every seventh day, which day is appropriately called the Lord's Day or Sunday. For on this day Christ's faithful are bound to come together into one place. They should listen to the word of God and take part in the Eucharist, thus calling to mind the passion, resurrection, and glory of the Lord Jesus, and giving thanks to God who "has begotten them again, through the resurrection of Christ from the dead, unto a living hope" (1 Pet 1:3). The Lord's Day is the original feast day, and it should be proposed to the faithful and taught to them so that it may become in fact a day of joy and of freedom from work.[5]

4. M. Herron, "Sunday and Holyday Observance," *The New Catholic Encyclopedia*, vol. 13 (New York: McGraw-Hill, 1967) 801.

5. All citations of Vatican II documents in this chapter are from the translation by Austin Flannery, O.P., in *Vatican Council II: The Conciliar and Post Conciliar Documents* (Collegeville, Minn.: The Liturgical Press, 1975).

The goal to which the Council calls us—so to celebrate the Lord's day "that it becomes in fact a day of joy and freedom from work"—is directly dependent upon how the assembly relates to the word and Eucharist it celebrates. Experience shows that it is possible to celebrate them in ways which leave the rest of the day untouched and empty. It is my concern here to explore how the Sunday celebration can turn our whole Sunday into a day of joy and freedom. After all, the Council claimed that the liturgy is "the primary and indispensable source from which the faithful are to derive the true Christian spirit" (CSL 14), and it was the model of the liturgy celebrated by the whole community on the Lord's Day that the Council had in mind (CSL 41-2).

In order to suggest how that "true Christian spirit" can be derived from the Sunday liturgy, I propose to approach the topic from four angles: 1) Preparation, 2) Participation, 3) Celebration, and 4) Integration. It is important to remember that these are four angles on the same subject and that while they represent a certain progression, each is in turn dependent upon all the others. Preparation, as we shall see, requires the kind of receptivity which we mean by "contemplation." Contemplative receptivity or attentiveness will in turn affect the way we participate, which in turn will be reflected in the quality of the celebration and will overflow the celebration itself, seeking to be integrated into the life of every day.

For the purposes of lending a certain concreteness to our reflections, let us suppose ourselves in the week between Trinity Sunday and Corpus Christi. Last Sunday, feast of the Blessed Trinity, brought us once again the story of God's love for us, a love so great that he gave his only Son, so that whoever believes in him may be saved to share in the life of the eternal God himself. The same tenderness and compassion, the same kindness and faithfulness, which our God displayed in speaking to Moses in a cloud on Sinai, has been revealed even more dramatically to us in the presence of the one he sent, Jesus the Lord. (See readings for Trinity Sunday.) As we turn to look forward to next Sunday, the feast of Corpus Christi proclaims and celebrates once again the kenotic love of the Lord: his being emptied out for our sakes in bread broken and blood poured, a total gift of himself to all of us who call him our Lord. "As I draw life from the Father, so whoever eats this bread, food indeed, and drinks this cup, drink indeed, draws life from me," says the Lord. "You live in me and I live in you." The one loaf we share forms a single body, the body of the crucified and risen one. (See readings for Corpus Christi.) Putting ourselves imaginatively between these two Sunday feasts, let us look at our position from the four angles we have proposed.

1. Preparation

Participation in the liturgy presupposes preparation for the liturgy; quality participation requires quality preparation. Such preparation is a matter of preparing a new ear with which to hear the new word of the Lord that will be spoken to us on Sunday. It means preparing the soil of the spirit to receive the word that will fall like seed from the hand of the sower and like gentle, nourishing rain. It is a matter of preparing the inner eye to receive new sight, of preparing the heart to hear with the inner ear.

How did we prepare ourselves, individually and as a community, to hear last Sunday's word? Were we present to God as Moses was in the cloud? Did we concern ourselves with Paul's exhortation to "try to grow perfect"? What would it mean to live each day in the life of Father, Son, and Spirit, as we claim we have begun to do in baptism? Perhaps our preparation fell short, so that now we have the hardest time remembering whether last Sunday's word said anything to us at all. If this is the case, what would we have to do to be prepared next Sunday?

In the spring I was visiting with my brother who is a dairy farmer sixty miles southwest of St. Louis. The drought of the past several years, he told me, had caused the subsoil to be very dry. Because of this, he had plowed the land as deeply as possible, so that it could drink up the precious winter moisture and so that the rains could penetrate deeply into the earth and counteract the effects of the long drought. By March, only two inches of rain had fallen. Still, farmers know what it is to wait: it is a fact of life for them. But they do not just wait—they wait in readiness. Believing that the rains would come, my brother went to harrow the fields and to ready them for the sowing.

I believe it is this kind of waiting in readiness that is lacking from our Sunday liturgy. By this I mean to include the people in the pews. We are all called to listen to the word, so we all need to be ready.

This waiting in readiness, I have suggested, is what is usually referred to as contemplation. Contemplation refers to a whole range of attitudes: listening, being really present to someone or something, being silent, being obedient in the etymological sense of *obaudire*, which means "bending one's ear to someone"—surrendering, being attentive, taking time, putting one's own spirit in tune with the Spirit of God, resting in the presence of the Lord. All this is implied in the work of contemplation, and its result is a heart receptive to the word of God, a word which, in the image of the prophet, is like "the rain and the snow [which] come down from heaven and return not thither but water the earth, making it bring forth and sprout . . ." (Isa 55:10-11).

Conversely, lack of preparation on the part of the assembly can only be compared to hardened, impenetrable, asphalt-like soil. The rain falls on it and runs off, leaving the seed of the word closed and sterile, changing little or nothing in the life of the individual or in the world. But it is not meant to be that way: "My word shall not return to me empty," says the Lord in the text cited above. Something is meant to happen! So how can we ready ourselves to let the word of God accomplish that purpose for which he sent it?

Working as I do in the diocese of Tulsa, Oklahoma, I have developed a simple process of preparing to hear the Sunday word, which I use with people who exercise ministries in the assembly. I regard these people as a priority, for their ministry is meant to flow out of the word, but of course the whole assembly is exercising a ministry and really needs to undertake the same kind of process.

As an example of how we might prepare ourselves to be hearers of the word, let us take the readings for the feast of Corpus Christi. We can begin with the Gospel Acclamation: "I am the living bread from heaven, says the Lord. Whoever eats this bread will live forever. Alleluia!" Remember, this acclamation is not merely a sneak preview or summary of the Gospel to be read. It is a sacramental word, proclaiming the presence among us of the Word-made-flesh, as we rise to our feet, joining the martyrs and saints as they stand, singing, before the throne of God and before the Lamb (Rev 7:9-12).

In preparing Sunday's liturgy, I strongly recommend beginning with the Gospel, for it is here that the heart of the day's message is to be found. So we would take John 6: 51-58 in preparing for Corpus Christi. We would hear it read through slowly. Individuals could take it in turns to repeat phrases that struck them and have stayed in their memory once the reading is over. This will serve to alert us to key phrases and images when we hear the reading again on Sunday. We can then proceed to read the first and second readings (Deut 8:2-3, 14b-16a and 1 Cor 10:16-17) in the same way. As this is done, we shall see how these readings shed light on the Gospel and are in turn illuminated by it.

Of course, this is only a beginning. It needs to be followed by some time of personal meditation on the word, so that each of us can be confronted by and drawn into prayer.

2. *Participation*

With such preparation, good participation in the Sunday liturgy is possible. I would suggest that it can no longer be considered the luxury of the devout few: it is a necessity for everyone in the assembly. As a result of having "wasted time" on such preparation, we will find that it already begins to affect the quality of our celebration from the very beginning, in the very act of gathering or assembling, even as we arrive and greet each other in the parking lot. If I have really sat down and meditated on the solemn assurance of the Lord that he is the living bread which gives us life, and confronted Paul's assertion that "we, though many, are one body because we all share in the one bread," this must affect my words and behavior. A wave or handshake or smile become the expression of the unity that is ours, a holy kiss shared among the saints, a sacrament of that same divine love which is poured out for us as our common food and drink.

With the sort of heightened sensitivity which contemplative preparation engenders in us, we shall find ourselves drawn much more easily into the flow of participation as we dare to welcome, assist, share with, and touch one another. In preparation, we find ourselves summoned and empowered to sing, struggle, respond, pray, process, carry and proclaim, confront, admit, bow, kneel, watch, listen— maybe even dance. We find ourselves remembering and forgiving, rejoicing and praising, eating and drinking, out of the deeper reality of the Lord himself, present in his assembly and in his word (CSL 7). On the other hand, we may be forced to ask ourselves whether this is indeed our experience. Perhaps the word bounces off us, its meaning eluding our grasp, drowned in the stream of words, words, words, which runs over us and away—because we are unprepared to let the word quench the thirst of our parched and hardened spirit.

3. Celebration

For a long time, I have been part of parish liturgy committees and have found myself engaged in evaluating each Sunday's liturgy and preparing for the next. In my experience, "good liturgy" has invariably been equated with the decibel factor of the singing. Likewise, my "success" as a liturgical minister has been judged by my ability—or lack of it—to conjure up a loud sound from the congregation, whether it be at the 8:00 A.M., the 11:00 A.M. or the Sunday evening liturgy. But there is more to it than that: for this reason I am introducing a distinction between participation and celebration.

Perhaps the distinction can best be understood if we take it as another form of the distinction between action and contemplation. The whole point is, of course, that while the two may be distinguished, they must not be separated, or else we are in trouble. There is an essential interplay between action and contemplation, between participation and celebration. We take the word of God to heart and let it come to new form in the celebration of our response—which is the response of the whole person, not just the sounds we make. Similarly with the Eucharistic acclamation: a celebration of Word-made-flesh, of food and drink made sacred. We celebrate the great Prayer of Thanksgiving by being personally present to the Lord and to the praying community. Our hearts as well as our voices go into the Great Amen at the conclusion of the Eucharistic Prayer. We celebrate peace flowing among us as the promised *shalom* of God permeates the assembly. We celebrate the one Lord in the one Body as we share the holy meal. We celebrate, i.e., live the reality of, the Church gathered into one, plunged into the saving passion, death, and rising of her Lord. We celebrate, in short, the reality that is coming to pass among us as we participate in the rite—but the expression on our faces usually reveals that we are unmindful of this truth.

We began by remarking that Sunday is the day of resurrection not merely in the sense that it was the day when something happened to Jesus (he was raised from the dead), but in the sense that it was the day when the first Christians recognized that something had happened to them—they had seen the Lord. Consequently, the primary proof of the resurrection was not the empty tomb, a later tradition,[6] but the experience of the assembled believers that "suddenly, without warning, Jesus stood before them and said, 'Peace'" (Matt 28:9). It thus marks the day after the end of the old world, "the day after the everyday world,"[7] when we recognize his presence in the community of believers, hear his voice speak in the reading of the Scriptures, recognize him again in the breaking of bread, and find ourselves challenged, like the servants at Cana, to "do what he tells you." The "sign" of water turned into wine is an image of the new age. At Mass, when we do what he told us to do, the eating of his broken and risen body and the drinking of his blood poured out for our saving, transform us in turn into signs of the new age. In Augustine's words, we receive what we are: the Body of Christ (Sermon 272). We are to become what we receive: the risen body of the crucified, evidence of God's victory over sin and death.

Unlike the six famous water pots, we are neither inanimate nor passive under the power of God's transforming word. The word does not override us: it calls us to be what it can make us. Hence our emphasis on preparing to hear the word. Each Sunday's liturgy, together with its prepara-

6. Raymond E. Brown, S.S., *The Virginal Conception and the Bodily Resurrection of Jesus* (New York: Paulist Press, 1973) 121.

7. Francis W. Nichols, "The Meaning of Sunday," *Today's Parish* (April 1981) 11.

tion, our participation, and its celebration, represents a call to plow deeply, to lay open the subsoil of the heart, that we might receive the word which is both seed and rain and which encompasses our death only to bring forth new life—the life of God himself. We know well enough that this is no sudden transformation: we cannot expect the sowing and the harvest to occur on the same day. The importance of the liturgical year is that it provides the opportunity for the continuing sowing and growth of the word in our lives. This, in turn, affects the quality of our celebration. As Kevin Seasoltz remarks in his book *New Liturgy, New Laws,* "No lasting liturgical progress is really possible without a biblical catechesis of the Christian community."[8]

An intelligent readiness to hear the word and to enter into its liturgical celebration thus brings with it a more willing and more conscious response to the celebration of the Eucharist. The ritualized action of word and Eucharist make the saving work of Christ the Lord present and effective for us in the assembled community,[9] so much so that we find ourselves literally standing within the presence of the mystery of Christ saving us, the paschal mystery of his death and resurrection. To participate in the celebration with faith is to put oneself into dying and rising with Christ in his Body which is the assembled Church. We are called to put our whole selves into this mystery, represented by the celebration of the liturgy. Without being prepared and ready, we can hardly expect to be able to give ourselves over—fully present in body, mind, and psyche—to this moment of spiritual opportunity.

From this perspective, we can see that Sunday and its observance is infinitely more than a practice to be legislated for. The law itself can be no more than an invitation to be-

8. R. Kevin Seasoltz, O.S.B., *New Liturgy, New Laws* (Collegeville, Minn.: The Liturgical Press, 1980) 10.
9. Thomas A. Krosnicki, S.V.D., Classnotes—The Liturgical Year, 1977.

come an Easter people, to be drawn into the mystery of Christ
and his mission of gathering into one the scattered children
of God. Sunday is the feast of the Lord personified in the
gathering of his faithful. It is the Lord personified in the
word proclaimed. It is the Lord personified in the meal we
share. The Sunday feast is the person of the Lord himself.[10]
The Lord is our Sunday celebration: our Sunday celebration
is the Lord.

4. Integration

It would be pointless to do what we do on Sundays if we
failed to integrate it with the rest of life. This, in fact, is the
commission we are given as the community is dismissed at
the end of the liturgy: the commission to integrate the saving
reality we have celebrated into the everydayness of our
lives. In the words of a Zen master: "Everyday life is the
path." This commissioning at the end of Mass echoes the
commission given to the women by Jesus on the first day of
the week: "Go, tell the brothers the news of my rising. Tell
them, I go before you into Galilee" (Matt 28:10). Galilee, of
course, was home for most of them: it was familiar territory,
the place where they lived and worked. Like Jesus, they
had come from Galilee and had brought with them their
peculiar accent and the experience of growing up and working there. Jesus spoke to them in terms of what they knew of
life: of marriage and childbirth, of farmers and fishermen,
of death and taxes.

   Our going up to Jerusalem for worship, for the experience of the dead and risen one, is likewise shaped by what
our experience in Galilee has taught us, by what we have
learned back home. What we bring to worship is what we
experience every day. Fr. Ed Hayes of Kansas City uses the
homely analogy of the potluck supper: it is what we bring

10. Patrick Regan, O.S.B., "The Fifty Days and the Fiftieth Day," *Worship* 55 (May 1981) 198.

to the liturgy that makes the occasion feast or famine. What we bring to the liturgy out of our week of living and working and preparing can enhance and challenge what we celebrate. In short, what we all bring to the liturgy is important for the impact it has upon us: it is a matter of being fully present —we, the assembly, Christ the Lord.

Conversely, the space between Sunday and Sunday is a space in which the word must be allowed to take flesh in the everydayness of our lives. If the word is really taken to heart, it will become the radical truth that bespeaks itself in the attitude we adopt towards everyday events. Really, it is a matter of Christian integrity. If we do not live out at home the "Amen" we pronounce in church, what does it mean to be a disciple of the Lord and of his Gospel? We must get to know the word, be confronted by it, struggle with its meaning, surrender to its transforming power.

The hope of transformation, of becoming "a new creation," is expressed by our going to Mass on the first day of the week, by the custom of wearing our "Sunday best," by the practice of cleaning house in preparation for Sunday guests, by making special efforts with Sunday dinner. During Easter week, I visited my mother and had taken along a hook rug that I was in process of finishing. It was of Indian design and used Oklahoma's colors. My mother said, "Surely you won't put this on the floor for people to walk on." When I said it was a gift and it would not be for me to say how it was used, she replied: "Well, perhaps on Sunday it could be used on the floor." The tradition of Sunday as a special day remains alive—the day of days that is freshest, best, and newest, for it is the dawn of a new creation, a new age, a new world, and a new hope.

Conclusion

How does the experience of encountering the risen Lord in the celebration of the liturgy—in assembly, word, and Eucharist—color and shape the general spirit of the day?

1. Sunday is the day on which we experience the Lord's rising and our rising in him—a call to a more profoundly personal dying and rising through a deeper appropriation of the Gospel.

2. Since we know that the Gospels were written from a post-resurrection viewpoint, we can be sure that the works of liberation which the Lord worked on the sabbath day— healing the sick, straightening the bent, enabling the blind to see, making the handicapped whole, and alleviating hunger —continued in the community of believers and should still be part of the observance of Sunday into the twenty-first century.

3. Sunday is the day when the gift of peace is given. Jesus' first word to his startled and guilty disciples on the first day of the week was *shalom* (peace). That same peace is offered to us in the liturgical assembly, and from there we take it home. But its indispensable precondition is laid down in Matthew 5:23-24: "If you bring your gift to the altar and there recall that your brother has anything against you, leave your gift at the altar, go first to be reconciled with your brother, and then come and offer your gift." Sunday is a day for making peace with our brothers and sisters.

4. Sunday is the day for breaking bread with the stranger invited to come and sit at our table. It is also the day for breaking open the word for a fuller understanding of the Scriptures. It is a day for being life-giving bread and living word to family, friends, and those in need.

5. Sunday is the day for encountering the risen Lord, even in the guise of a gardener or a companion along the way, or in the blind, the crippled, the lonely, the unexpected —as the women discovered when they went to the tomb. It is also a day for putting fingers into wounds and discovering the reality of the resurrection of the crucified one.

6. Sunday is also a day of mission. It is the day when we become conscious of the Lord's commission to make disciples

of all nations, baptizing them and making known to them all that he has commanded us.

7. Finally, Sunday is also the day on which the gift of the Spirit of God was poured out on the disciples as they were assembled for prayer. For us, too, our Sunday assembly is the occasion of our being empowered from on high with the personal love-gift of the Father and the risen Son.

All this may sound like an enormous agenda for Sunday, but there are two things which need to be said about it. First, it all amounts to no more than fidelity to one's baptismal promises, which are the normal and ordinary way to holiness and which were modeled for us in the life-style of Jesus himself. The life-style of Jesus was characterized above all by a sensitive awareness of people and places, fields and flowers; by a ministry marked by truthfulness and compassion; by being true to himself in all his relationships, true to himself as the radiant and exact reflection of the Father's being (Heb 1:3).[11] The second point simply refines the first. It is that Sunday rest is not a matter of taking a rest or passing the day in idleness. Nor are we suggesting it should be passed in a frenzy of activity. The observance of Sunday calls us to live more profoundly the life-style of Jesus by being deeply present for and to those about us, and by being willing to receive the gift of the other person into our lives in a way that challenges us to Easter action. It is about acting contemplatively.

Let me conclude with an Easter meditation of one of our Tulsa priests:

> When we proclaim, "He is risen,"
> we mean more than victory over the grave.
>
> We are saying he has saved life
> from disintegrating into sadness and sin.

---

11. Wilkie Au, S.J., "Lay Ministry and Gospel Living," *Ministries* 2 (April 1981) 7–8.

We are saying that Easter is the free
and gracious breakthrough of God's love
into the brokenness of human life.

We are saying Jesus' resurrection
transforms the irreversible darkness of death
into new life.

We are saying Jesus broke the chains of death forever
and arose in an earthquake of sunlight.
It was an earthquake in human consciousness
which reversed forever
the downward spiral of violence and despair.

We are saying that light is stronger than darkness
that life is stronger than death
and goodness is stronger than all the forces of iniquity.

We will experience redemption and resurrection
when we understand what the Risen Lord
told Mary of Magdala:
"Tell them, I go before you into Galilee.
There you will see me."[12]

12. James McGlinchey, *Eastern Oklahoma Catholic*, Easter 1981 (adapted).

Sunday Morning:
Retrospect and Prospect

GODFREY DIEKMANN, O.S.B.

Like Caesar's Gaul, and like all well-constructed meditations, this paper is divided into three parts: what Sunday has been like in the past; what its present state is; what it will probably be in the future.

I. Sunday in the Past

In the interests of decent brevity, I shall speak only of the past which I personally knew and experienced before Vatican II. The first characteristic of this past, as I remember it, was that Sunday observance meant Sunday obligation, a personal obligation binding on every Catholic under pain of mortal sin. To fulfill this obligation one had to be physically present

---

GODFREY DIEKMANN, a monk of St. John's Abbey in Collegeville, Minnesota, served on the preparatory commission that prepared the Vatican II Constitution on the Sacred Liturgy, and is a founder and lifetime member of the International Commission on English in the Liturgy. He holds a doctorate in theology and is professor of patristics at St. John's University in Collegeville, Minnesota, and The Catholic University of America in Washington, D.C. Editor in chief of *Worship* since 1938, he is internationally known as a lecturer on liturgy, and recently received the Berakah Award from the North American Academy of Liturgy.

at the three principal parts of the Mass—the offertory, the sacrifice, and the Communion. Notice that the Liturgy of the Word was not covered by this obligation: Scripture was expendable. Moreover, I can honestly say that before Vatican II there was no stress whatever on the theology of the assembly—I doubt whether I even heard the term before the 1950s. Since Sunday Mass attendance was above all a matter of the individual's personal obligation, the essentially social and communitarian character of the Eucharist was rarely adverted to, even though it is the unanimous teaching of Scripture and most of the Tradition. In those days, people would have been startled by the declaration of the third-century *Didascalia Apostolorum* (ch. 13): "Now when thou teachest, command and warn the people to be constant in assembling in church and not to withdraw themselves, but always to assemble lest any person diminish the church by not assembling and cause the body of Christ to be short a member."

They would also have been puzzled by St. Augustine's succinct summary of Eucharistic theology, namely, that the Church not merely confects the Eucharist, but the Eucharist in turn confects the Church. I know what a revelation that was for me personally. I had studied the *Summa Theologica* sixteen hours a week and still remember vividly what a discovery it was when I found that St. Thomas Aquinas' principal Eucharistic theme was *res huius sacramenti est unitas mystici corporis* (the grace [the purpose, the effect] of the sacrament is the unity of the Mystical Body). The Eucharist is the chief celebration by which we become what we are. It is a celebration of the Church becoming a community of faith and love, or, as I like to express it, the Church becoming event.

But almost none of this was taught or understood. One result of this was that the newly introduced kiss of peace became one of the chief stumbling blocks of the liturgical reform, and opposition to it remains to this day a major plank of traditionalist Catholics. In the June 18, 1981, edition of

The Wanderer, one of its columnists, Frank Morriss, wrote in an editorial attack on Archbishop Rembert Weakland, chairman of the Bishops' Committee on the Liturgy: "Archbishop Weakland thinks that Americans are a wee bit inhibited when it comes to the kiss of peace. Did he ever think that a majority found it disturbing? Archbishop Weakland says that some lectors speak to us as if we were ignoramuses. Why does he not consider that the so-called kiss of peace treats us likewise, for it summons us down from heaven to the everyday." Such an attitude, curious as it may seem, still operates unconsciously in many people, including many priests who seem to feel they were ordained to offer sacrifice whether there is a congregation or not. This is not unlike the surgeon who feels he has to operate, just to keep his hand in, whether the patient needs it or not. In the conviction of many liturgists, it is precisely this mentality which offers the greatest obstacle to liturgical renewal: the "my-Mass" mentality. A celebrant who thinks in these terms can hardly do justice on a Sunday to the basic principle that it is the whole *ecclesia* which offers. The whole Church offers—not just the priest offering, with the people joining him.

A second characteristic of the preconciliar Sunday was the separation between sacrifice and Communion. Since the Council of Trent there had been such an emphasis on sacrifice that the Communion of the people had become expendable. Sung Mass, High Mass, Solemn Mass—so far as I know none of them ever had Communion for the people. There is a legend told at St. John's Abbey, Collegeville, concerning Senator Eugene McCarthy. While he was a student at St. John's, he is reputed to have called out at a Sunday High Mass, "Open the tabernacle!" And that was considered an unreasonable demand on his part because there had been a Communion Mass earlier which he could have attended. If I am not mistaken, there was a special rubric which forbade the distribution of Holy Communion at pontifical Masses.

In 1956, I attended the landmark international pastoral-liturgical conference held at Assisi. The program there carried the instruction that no one was to receive Communion at the papal Mass. At Vatican II, it was not until the Third Session that provision was made for the laity to receive Communion at the daily conciliar Mass. To all intents and purposes, Communion for the people was expendable in modern times, a condition which was only slightly alleviated by Pius X's decree on frequent and early Communion promulgated in 1905.

Third, what was the standing of Sunday in the Catholic mind? It was the day decreed by the Church for the fulfillment of our Mass obligation, the day on which the bloody sacrifice of the cross was renewed in an unbloody manner. But there was no hint of Sunday as an Easter celebration, though this was clear as crystal in the documents of the Church's early tradition, such as Justin Martyr and the *Didascalia*. That Sunday Mass was a celebration of the Lord's resurrection had long since been forgotten. It was back in the 1920s that there was the first faint inkling that Sunday might have something to do with resurrection; but in the forties and fifties, the liveliest theological discussion centered on the question of whether the resurrection had a salvific effect. We were saved by the death of Christ, everyone seemed to think, and the resurrection was something that happened afterwards, a miraculous event that proved his divinity and so assured us of the infinite value of his sacrificial death. What probably did more than anything else to change people's understanding was the publication of Durwell's book on the resurrection. It wasn't until 1960 that it was available in English, and it was only then that Sunday and resurrection began to be reassociated in people's minds.

One is forced to ask oneself how the salvific role of the resurrection could ever have become so forgotten. Historians offer various hypotheses, but this is mine, for what it is worth. Originally, every Sunday was a day of resurrection, or, rather, it was the summation of the whole paschal mystery of Christ's suffering and death climaxing in the resurrection. Then, in the second century, came the feast of Easter. I have as yet been unable to discover precisely when Easter was introduced into the West. I am personally convinced that when the great Polycarp of Smyrna came to Rome to discuss the celebration of Easter with Bishop Anicetus, about the year 152 A.D., the question was not on what date the feast should be celebrated, but whether there should be an annual feast at all. This seems the only sensible way of interpreting the description of their meeting given by Eusebius in bk. V, ch. 24, of his *Ecclesiastical History*. Polycarp and the Christians of Asia Minor had obviously been celebrating Easter for some time. Rome, as always throughout history, was conservative in matters theological and liturgical and was unwilling to change. If this hypothesis is correct, Easter was not yet known as an annual festival at Rome in the middle of the second century. However, by the time of Pope Victor, about 180 A.D., and his struggle with Polycrates of Asia Minor, the case was quite different. Rome and its allies were now insisting that Easter always be celebrated on a Sunday. The Asian Christians, the so-called Quartodecimans, insisted on their Jewish-based tradition of celebrating the Christian Passover on 14 Nisan, i.e., on a fixed calendar date, no matter on what day of the week it fell. The Quartodecimans were a rather small minority and soon the Roman position prevailed. The result was that the universal Church now had the great, unique, important feast of Easter, the summation of all Sundays. This annual feast became the climax of the year, a day so important that it soon overshadowed all other Sundays and obscured their original connection with the resurrection "on the first day of the week." Sundays then ended up as days dedicated to the mystery of the Trinity, days on which every Catholic was obliged to worship, days when, paradoxically, we immortalized Christ's saving death, which occurred on a Friday.

II. SUNDAY IN THE PRESENT

In talking of Sunday in the present, I mean Sunday since Vatican II. I have often been accused of being an incorrigible optimist, but in this instance I feel certain that facts justify my positive judgment about the results of Vatican II as far as Sunday celebration of the Eucharist is concerned. Sociologists are, I believe, unanimous in declaring that human beings are generally most conservative and opposed to change in matters that concern worship, especially public worship. They insist on clinging to customs whose meaning has long since been forgotten. It is all the more astonishing, then, that every major scientific survey made in the United States concerning the changes in the liturgy has met with a high percentage of favorable votes, ranging from 70 percent upwards—a fact one would not suspect from the persistent and often strident minority protest in some sections of the press. Moreover, since most of our people who participate in liturgy do so on Sundays, it is with the Sunday situation in mind that most of the liturgical changes have been introduced into our parishes. In general, I think, we are going in the right direction and moving at a pace which, by all sociological standards, is astounding. A major factor keeping us on the right track, I am sure, is the remarkably large and ever increasing number of priests, religious, and laity who are receiving expert training and academic degrees in such places as Notre Dame. This became evident a few years ago when the North American Academy of Liturgy was founded as a professional society for trained liturgists. It already numbers several hundred members. I cannot cover all the changes affecting Sunday liturgy since Vatican II, but five points are especially significant.

1. The Actual Celebration of Sunday. Much has been accomplished, but much remains to be done. The most urgent need we have is for a *systematic training of the clergy*. What is at stake here is a radical reorientation of our thinking with regard to the role of the ordained priesthood in sacrificial worship, something which cannot be achieved just by good-will or a few institutes or some spiritual pep talks during a retreat. Vatican II insists upon the essential distinction between the priesthood of the ordained minister and that of the laity. This is well and good, but I wish there could have been equal insistence, and not just a mere statement, that despite this essential difference, both the priesthood of the ordained and the priesthood of the holy People of God are merely different manners of sharing the one and only priesthood of Christ. The constant teaching of the Church up to the twelfth century was simply *ecclesia offert* (the Church offers). This remains true even if it is also true that different people in the Church have different liturgical roles. (The article by Hervé-Marie Legrand, "The Presidency of the Eucharist according to the Ancient Tradition," *Worship* 53 (1979) 413–438, is very revealing on this point.) I suspect that the average ordained priest in the United States still thinks, unwittingly if not consciously, in pre–Vatican II terms: namely, "I have been chosen by God and consecrated to offer sacrifice, and my people must now be urged to join their action with mine, that is, to offer with and through me." Hence, for so many, the enduring scandal of finding Justin, about 165 A.D., calling the chief celebrant "president" instead of "priest."

Of course, the clergy are often abetted in such attitudes in ways that are both subtle and difficult to change. One thinks of the architectural arrangement and structure of our churches which have such lasting and pervasive influence. As Bob Rambusch keeps reminding us, since Vatican II at least 90 percent of the time and effort given to church renovation has gone into the rearrangement of the sanctuary, while the body of the church has remained relatively unaffected. Was it not, perhaps, one of the unrecognized tragedies of liturgical history that the Church, particularly the Western Church, once freed from persecution, accepted as the model of its public worship-space the plan of the contemporary secular basilica? It offered a long, narrow area into which an elevated section could easily be introduced for the president of the assembly, thereby creating an unmistakable spatial division which could and did contribute mightily to the growing class distinction between clergy and laity. I, for one, heartily wish we could declare a moratorium—the longer the better—on the two words *shepherd* and *head* as applied to bishop and priest. The basilica church, and its successors in Romanesque, Gothic, and Baroque, shout "headship"; they are designed for a priest who dominates, who does everything that matters on his own, including, of most importance, the offering of sacrifice. Finally, the holy People of God were barred even from seeing what was going on at the altar by the erection of the rood-screen! Thank God, we are at last beginning radically to rethink our Sunday worship space, so that the president can once again be seen as just that, the symbol of unity whose chief task it is to form an actively worshiping congregation or community.

2. Sunday as an Easter Celebration. I would be the last to deny that the rediscovery of the Easter character of Sunday has been a force for revitalization. Once we had almost entirely forgotten that the Mass is a resurrection service; now we are surrounded by banners with their inevitable proclamation of life and joy! Certainly, it needed emphasizing to redress the imbalance of the past, but now things have almost reached the point where, if you don't feel like rejoicing or greeting your neighbor at the kiss of peace with a warm smile, then sheer honesty and integrity would seem to sug-

gest that you stay away. Is this the necessary consequence of recovering the resurrection? Notice that the Constitution on the Sacred Liturgy (106) speaks of the Mass as celebrating the *paschal mystery* each Sunday: not only the Lord's resurrection and glorification, but also his passion. I am afraid we have in the course of these few short years almost forgotten that that is so, and we have some more readjustments to make, both in theory and practice. The ancient axiom *per crucem ad lucem* (through the Cross to light) is still valid, both spiritually and psychologically.

3. Vatican II also reminded us that the purpose of the Eucharistic celebration goes beyond simply providing for the sum total of the personal devotional needs and spiritual obligations of those present. Rather, the first and basic purpose of the Sunday celebration is the formation of a community of faith and love, so that thereby—by the formation of the *ecclesia*—God might be glorified. It is the formation of a community which gives glory to God. But, according to Plato, community presupposes at the very least the possibility of personal acquaintance and the experience of relations of goodwill. This is one instance in which I am almost inclined to become a pessimist! About 70 percent of American Catholics live in urban areas where, according to one wit, the chief pastoral-liturgical problem is the adequacy of the parking lot on Sundays. Already more than forty years ago, Karl Sonnenschein, a Catholic sociologist from Berlin, declared that the chief mortal sin in today's Catholic Church is the large city parish, which even God, he said, could not transform into a community with his sacrament of unity. As an American bishop put it a few years ago: the chief cause of leakage in the United States is Mass every hour on the hour. Fortunately, more and more priests are aware of the problem and are trying to do something about it; and *that*, I would say, is one of the major achievements of the Council's document on the liturgy.

4. If I were asked what, in fact, had been the chief results of the post–Vatican II liturgical reforms, I think I would be inclined to give pride of place to the fact that many thousands of non-clerics are now personally involved in the planning and execution of the Sunday liturgy. Whereas the Sunday Mass was once a solo performance, the people are now becoming involved, *mirabile dictu,* even in the homily. Much has been accomplished. Justin, in the year 160, speaks for the first time of lectors; Hippolytus, half a century later, adds a few more kinds of ministers; but I doubt whether there was ever a time in the entire history of the Church when there was such a variety and number of non-clerical Eucharistic ministers as we have today—and this despite what I said earlier about the still all-too-prevalent clerical mindset concerning the Eucharistic sacrifice.

5. By way of a concluding footnote: whenever I read that we have just about finished with the externals of Vatican II liturgical reforms and that now we can finally begin to interiorize these reforms, making them spiritually meaningful and fruitful, I am afraid I become just a trifle annoyed. I have no right to judge others, but as for myself, if liturgical renewal since the mid-1920s had implied chiefly external changes in ritual or architecture or whatever, I for one would not have wasted my life's efforts on it—and I am sure I speak for all the old pioneers.

III. Sunday in the Future

I know as little about the future as the next person, but since the sponsors of this Conference have asked me to play the prophet, I will try, briefly, to comply. I can only repeat what I have stated already: given the present discipline of the Church, we are soon going to be faced with an insoluble and disastrous situation. Owing to the growing shortage of ordained priests, it is safe to venture a guess that already at

the present time, nearly a third of the Catholics of the world
—perhaps more—are unable to attend Sunday Mass.

New statistics bombard us almost daily. The *Christian
Century*, in an article on the Church in France (June 3–10
[1981] 646), tells us that the ordination of priests nosedived
from 1,649 in 1965 to only 99 in 1977, and that more than
a thousand parishes in France are without clergy. The diocese
of Rome last year ordained four men to serve four million
people! Were it not for the many foreign priests living in
the Roman monasteries and universities, the faithful of
Rome would be among the most neglected Christians in
the world. I spent the spring semester of 1981 in Washington, D.C., where I lived with a priest who, while serving as
a pastor in his native Nigeria, had to take care of *forty* missions! The situation of many areas of South America, Africa,
and the Far East is similar. Crosier Bishop Sowada, native
of the diocese of St. Cloud and now ordinary of a diocese in
Indonesia, wrote recently that only 20 percent of his people
could be present for Sunday Mass. Yet Rome keeps firmly
to the policy of ordaining only celibate clergy. For instance,
in a letter to the Brazilian hierarchy (quoted in the *National
Catholic Reporter*, June 19, 1981), Rome once again repeated
that the answer to the priest shortage is not to be looked for
in the abolition of priestly celibacy or the ordination of married men or the return to ministry of priests who have married. (Notice that it doesn't say a word about the ordination
of women!) As a theologian, I happen to disagree with Rome
on all the reasons alleged in support of such a stance. I consider the position of Rome to be disciplinary in character
and thus destined ultimately, as the Indonesian bishops
pointed out in asking for a married clergy, to cede to the
more basic right of Christian people to participate regularly
in the celebration of the Eucharist.

To this I would add a second reason which, I believe, has
hardly been mentioned in the endless discussion about this

matter. This is the right of people to experience Christian community, to be actively and responsibly engaged in becoming part, not just of a parish but of a community of loving and caring brothers and sisters in Christ which, by divine dispensation, is accomplished in the eating and drinking of the same bread and the same cup. Witness Paul's words: "We, though many, are one body because we partake of the one bread." If there is one great lesson of Christian renewal today which stands out above all others, it is the one being taught us by South America. The Christians of South America are teaching us that community can be best and most effectively accomplished through Christian renewal in small groups, in *communidades de base*. So where does that leave our large city parish? We might guess that something like 30 percent of our people are physically unable to be present at Sunday Mass and that, of the remaining 70 percent, a large proportion cannot participate fully and properly, as spiritually integrated members of a community, because of the character of Sunday Mass in our city parishes. They are prevented from experiencing the kind of community to which they have a right to belong.

This seems like a very bleak picture. It may seem less bleak, however, when we remember that in the very springtime of the Church, a rather similar situation prevailed. Justin, writing from Rome about the year 160, describes in his first Apology the Sunday celebration of Eucharist. The reason for celebrating on this day is quite explicit: "Jesus Christ our Savior rose from the dead on this day." He goes on to say that "on the day called Sunday there is a meeting in one place of all those who live in the city or in the country." I am convinced that scholars have consistently misinterpreted that phrase, as if it meant that practically the whole community managed to meet together for the celebration of the Eucharist on Sundays. But we have to remember that Sunday was not a work-free day, a day of leisure, at that time, and that most Christians belonged to the lower strata of society. They were not masters of their own time and, even if they could make it to the common worship assembly, they would be subject to denunciation and persecution if they were found out. So I honestly doubt whether these people that gathered from the city and the country represented anything more than a slim minority of the total membership of the local church. Justin was expressing an ideal. His subsequent remark that the consecrated elements were carried by deacons to those unable to attend may well imply, not just a few absentees but a large percentage, even a majority, of the community. For those absentees, receiving the consecrated elements from the deacons meant nothing less than their participation in the communal Eucharistic celebration of the Sunday.

This evidence must prompt us to ask ourselves whether perhaps we have not through the centuries placed so much emphasis on the sacrifice—often for apologetic reasons—that we have forgotten the words of Paul in 1 Cor 11:26: "Every time you eat this bread and drink this cup, you are proclaiming the death of the Lord until he comes." Or, as we affirm in one of the acclamations, "When we eat this bread and drink this cup we proclaim your death, Lord Jesus, until you come in glory." Nothing is said about the sacrificial Eucharistic prayer! I am not entirely sure of the ramifications of this line of thought, but it seems to me to be one we can no longer ignore, and it fits in rather well with the evidence described by Jean Leclercq in his article on "Eucharistic Celebrations Without Priests In the Middle Ages" in *Worship*, March 1981.

There is a second line of thought which may also be relevant to the problem of the critical shortage of priests under the present discipline, but which should at least give theologians—and maybe Rome itself—something to ponder. Hippolytus, writing at Rome in about the year 215, describes in his *Apostolic Tradition* the ordination of bishops, presbyters, and deacons. But then in chapter 9 he goes on to say: "If a confessor (i.e., one who has suffered for the faith, a living martyr) has been in prison for the name of the Lord, you do not lay hands on him for the office of presbyter or deacon. He has the office of presbyter in virtue of his confession. If, however, he is to be ordained bishop, hands are to be laid on him." Here we have what might be called a charismatic yet true presbyterate without laying-on of hands, allowing the person to preside at Eucharist as authentically as if he had been ordained in the normal fashion. And Hippolytus was no extremist! On the contrary, he was what I would be inclined to characterize as the Cardinal Ottaviani of his time, for he wrote his treatise precisely to restrain ecclesiastical innovators in his day.

What has been done once can be done again. If we apply the rule of Hippolytus to the situation of my Nigerian friend with his forty missions, we could ask whether, given the spiritual need arising from deprivation of the Eucharistic celebration, the outlying communities might not be entitled to choose from among their members a presiding priest, one to whom God has clearly given the gift of leadership. I ask the question; I do not know the answer.

Perhaps all this is a dream, but does not Scripture itself allow young men to have visions and old men to dream dreams? Nevertheless, I regard it not as a dream, but as a matter of pastoral-liturgical realism that we should promote the ideal of Sunday Eucharist while retaining the utmost flexibility. I have given more talks on the Easter character of Sunday than anyone I know, yet I heartily applaud the extension of the Sunday celebration to Saturday evening. At the National Liturgical Week held some years ago at Princeton, the topic was once again Sunday worship. I argued then—and I was in a minority—that the term *Sunday worship* should be interpreted so as to include the whole weekend, starting on Friday night. That, I believe, would be a realistic response to the sociological conditions prevailing in America today. In any case, the paschal mystery we celebrate in the Eucharist includes the death of the Lord, which took place on a Friday. Sunday is for people, not people for the Sunday. In other circumstances—for example, when a priest has many missions to attend to or, in this country, where people are pleading for smaller worship groups—I would consider whichever day the priest may manage to celebrate with them to be Sunday. For Christians, Sunday is not primarily the calendrical first day of the week, but the day for the common celebration of the paschal mystery.

"The liturgy is for man, not man for the liturgy." These were the liberating words of Cardinal Montini, later Pope Paul VI, in one of the opening sessions of Vatican II. Let us never forget these words in any planning of liturgical celebration, including the hitherto untouchable sacredness of the Sunday Eucharistic assembly. If we do forget them, if we cling to past practices, however beautiful or meaningful or ideal, instead of keeping uppermost in our minds the changing needs of the People of God, the Church will become a museum piece. It will simply self-destruct. And God forbid that that should happen, or that we should have to have the responsibility for such an end upon our consciences.

The Mathis Award: Response

GODFREY DIEKMANN, O.S.B.

I appreciate the honor of this award all the more because this year marks not only the tenth anniversary of the Notre Dame Center for Pastoral Liturgy June Conference, but also the fiftieth anniversary of my ordination to the priesthood. The past fifty years have certainly had their ups and downs, so let the dead bury the dead and let us look forward to the next fifty years! I am deeply and humbly grateful as I accept this prestigious award, not for any merits I may have in the pastoral-liturgical field, for they are small, indeed, but because the award will, I hope, contribute to the association of my name with that of Fr. Michael Mathis, C.S.C., who has been one of the great heroes of my life.

Looking over this assembly, I am inclined to believe that with the exception, perhaps, of Lucy McCullough, I knew him better than anyone else here. I have the honor to have been his friend and a collaborator with him from the beginning in the realization of the primacy of the liturgical apostolate in the life of the Church. As some of you no doubt know, the discovery of the liturgy and of its centrality in the life of the Church was something that Father Michael came to discover only in the middle years of his life. His training was in missiology. His liturgical achievements were those of a self-made man, but the fact is that once he had realized the unique role of the liturgy in Christian life and piety, nothing—and I mean *nothing*—could stop him from devoting his life to the cause. I believe it was this unmistakable singleness of purpose, together with his almost naive optimism that there could be no major obstacle because this was God's cause, that charmed and attracted the succession of great liturgical scholars from Europe who graced and distinguished the summer schools at Notre Dame even in the earliest years: Jungmann, Bouyer, Balthasar Fischer, and many others. These were the *crème de la crème* of Europe, the ones who were soon to compose the document eventually promulgated by Vatican II as the Constitution on the Sacred Liturgy.

Michael Mathis was ever the genial host. Whenever you visited him in his room, he invariably just happened to find a bottle of Greek Metaxa—resinated wine—forgetting he had found the same bottle for you just ten days ago. Perhaps his greatest joy, apart from the celebration of the Eucharist, was to help choose and co-chair the hundred American delegates to the 1956 International Pastoral Liturgical Congress at Assisi. That congress represented what one might call the first public flexing of muscles on the part of the hitherto still largely suspect "litniks." In fact, the Congress was actually sanctioned by Rome itself.

Then there was Michael Mathis the liturgist, a man so full of his subject, the liturgy of the Church, that he never knew when or how to stop talking about it. Anyone who ever attended his famous daily matins services will look back to them with love and exasperation in almost equal measure. The faithful ones—John Julian Ryan and his wife, Mary Perkins Ryan, the Nuttings, the Bucks, Lucy McCullough, Mama Gurian, and half-a-dozen others, sometimes as many as twenty or thirty—came because they loved Father Michael. They knew he was correct in his prayer principles, but they were simply unable to shorten his half-hour (or longer) commentary on the readings. When chided about it, he admitted guilt and promised amendment, but the very next day he simply forgot all about it, especially if the readings were wildly allegorical.

I came to visit him and to be edified by him when he was confined to a hospital bed in what was his terminal illness. I was present, too, among the extraordinarily cheerful mourners at his funeral. Dear Michael Mathis, my beloved brother, I look forward to seeing you before long in the heavenly liturgy, and to hearing you expatiate at length (how else?) on your most recent discovery, the full meaning of Origen's commentary on the Song of Songs, chapter seven!